Printed by LULU.com USA 2013

Filanpine Press and Publishing 2013

# Thoughts in Rhyme ©

An anthology of poems written over many years, as expressions of thoughts on those subjects which lay in one's mind, about which one can do little to alter.

## Author


## Phillip A Robbins



Filanpine Press and Publishing 2013



robbinsrest@sky.com

Cover photo:- Taken by mistake.

Snapped a quick shot of a church in 'Lymington high street,' late one afternoon. Then forgot to wind 'on' the film in my old box camera.

Not an hour later, at sunset, took a photo of the view across the Solent towards 'Mudford Quay' near Christchurch in Dorset.



robbinsrest@sky.com

# Thoughts in Rhyme

Phillip Anthony Robbins

An anthology of poems: Recording my deepest thoughts; on all manner of subjects. Strange how one can learn so much about one's own understanding, morals and desires from the subconscious mind, provoked by events which effect and churn up the senses.

The thing is, do these have any interest or power for other souls?

Are they just empty mumblings? or have they captured something of value which may actually be of interest when shared? I do hope so.

It is certainly true that these poems leave me feeling vulnerable and exposed. Initially weakened, then slowly heartened, independent and strong.

May God bless you and bring His will for your lives, may the daily grind be only the vehicle upon which you travel to an enlightened happy understanding of how wonderful His creations earth and life really are.

These Poems have been written over almost forty years, inspired by those things which awake or stir my senses. Then in most cases some unseen force takes over, I am reluctant to take full credit for those which people have kindly said, Are 'wonderful' or 'inspired'. Many are beyond my own capability in the use of English vocabulary, which raises a few questions I am unable to answer as yet or offer reasonable explanation for.

All this aside, I find I am often 'driven' to express myself in this fashion. The first draft often has content, topic, resolution and expression beyond anything I can coldly just sit and scribble. Perhaps under this feeble frame and accumulated assortment of practical skills, there is an untapped intelligence which fights to express itself in my deeper subconscious.

This only succeeds when I am tired, vulnerable, moved or forced to be still. My 'driven,' 'Hyper manic,' tendencies have mostly worked for me in all practical aspects. After some health issues in the early 90s, that is the 1990s, I was only in my early 40s.

This personality trait, began to work against me and I was forced to seek other means of achieving the drive and energy to get through every day. Depression and poor physical health rather slows one down and enables a degree of self-assessment, which is a frightening learning curve.

All these issues are just 'chapters,' small events in the larger scale which is what we call 'our life'. They either break you or you form tough scars and endeavor to proceed with care. On new paths, in fresh directions, whilst hoping to retain your sensitivity, compassion and understanding without ever becoming vulnerable, stupid or hardened. Life is just too precious and exciting to permit anything to steal our ability to fully embrace it. These are just one man's thoughts on things which have moved or incensed, awoken an emotion outside of his immediate ability to comprehend.

Writing down these assembled words eventually relieves the tension and seems to enable expression of the frustration. A psychological release; enabling retention, of a degree of sanity. From my own perspective anyway.

The poems will undoubtedly reveal something of my deeper self, which may either, weaken or strengthen my standing amongst acquaintance's and strangers alike. I no longer care if this makes me look weak, as I have discovered in my fifties, I finally have the strength to cope with it.

They are designed to be **read aloud**; or **performed** with '**practiced intonation** and **delivery**'. Even emphasis **on some theatrics** on occasion.

Phillip Anthony Robbins

**Filanpine press & Publishing 2013**

I was very honoured after 5 years of study in my mid-40s to be awarded, 'Adult student for 1996' at Petworth house. Local paper came and took photos with some of the 16 books in which my poetry had appeared.

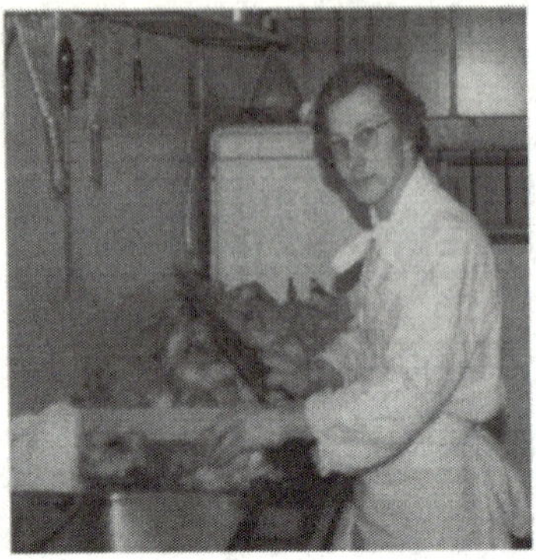

Chef saucier aged 19

Globe Hotel Queensgate

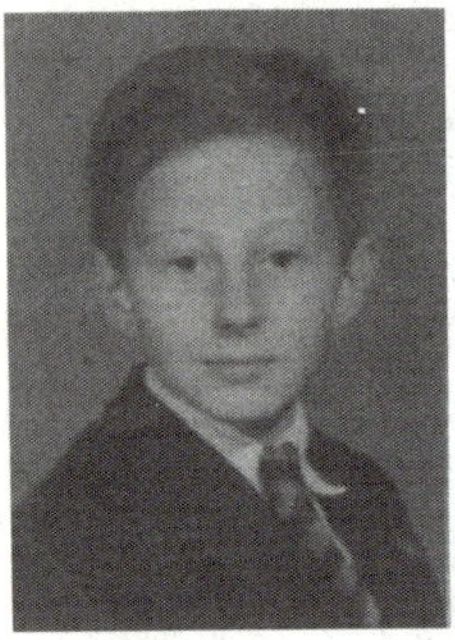

Gorringe Park secondary for boys. Phillip aged 11 in 1964

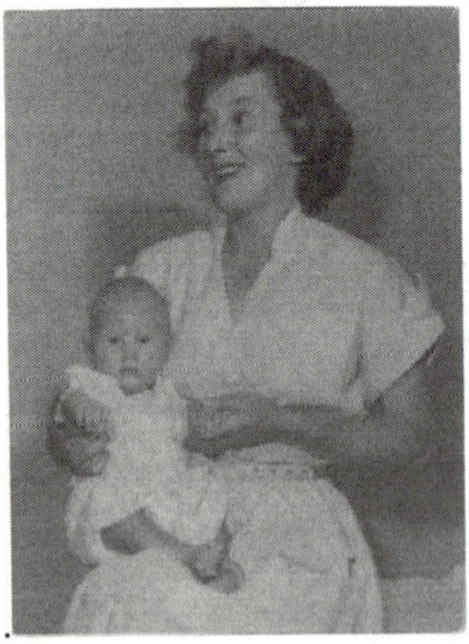

Me and my Mother, Doreen 1953

## Index of Thoughts in Rhyme ©

Page

66. Mirrors of Your Love
67. Ignorant market ( Folk Song )
68. Silent awe
69. Sold out
70. Song thrush
71. Street cred
72. Sophie ( For Miss S Bassett )
73. Starlite Nights ( Our Band )
75. Temporary profit
77. The Few and You
80. Waters Meet
81. Welcome End
82. Yet I See Him
84. Horse
85. Growing Love
88. Fifties and counting
91. Relief
94. Musical Solution
95. Man ( Very Green )
98. True values
99. Fear, Trust and Love.
100. Reoccurring smile
101. Avoid this mistake
103. Lighthouse Beam ( For Phil Birchenough 2012 )
105. Unfailing beauty
106. Cross to Bare
107. Thank you Emmanuel
108. Redeeming light
109. Beautiful Planet, and yet!
110. Judge and Assess
111. My little 'Bruvver' ( Best Mans speech )
113. Emotive news ( For Cecile )
115. Foretold, forgiven, saved
118. Such as Eve
119. Winter companions
120. If I were Irish ( Only my thoughts )
123. The waves
126. Graceful, ungraceful
127. Our 'Enry! (Sing with Henry Cooper )
129. Johnson (Death Row )
130. Trilogy (Water, Ice & Steam )

Phillip A Robbins

Published by Filanpine Press and Publishing

Printed by LULU.com USA

**Published by Filanpine Press and Publishing**

## Old Man's Rant

What a diverse world we have become,
This makes us special, harder to overcome.
Like some essential machine,
With parts designed for a specific task…
Coming together to function; in their given part.
We've come to a point now, a cross roads it's sure,
Where some things are being taken; perhaps too far.
Celebrating, 'witchcraft,' magic and the extreme,
Over painted, studded and tattooed as a theme.
As a minority in the mix, adding colour and some spice,
Wonderful until it's your own daughter's choice in life.
Coming into schools younger than twelve,
With tattoos, studs and imagine it's all new,
Standing out, thinking their special or seen as 'Cool'.
As with smoking, lost virginity and other things,
They all become badges to wear, like 'nose rings'.
The urge to be special, like all their friends…
Peer pressure, compliance, acceptance,
To be liked, begin to be the same, to fit in…
This all becomes a powerful curse or hex,
I am so grateful, the only way is not Essex.
If we become all the same, oh what a shame,
How do we stop this? Who do we blame?
Like the machine with identical parts,
Would only be suitable for one single task,
So many other wonderful traits will be missed,
So much in diversity, would no longer exist.
November 2012

**The Candle**

The candlelight; it flickers,
Throwing shadows up the wall.
In every shade imaginable, vivid, stark they fall.
Spooky, in the evenings when one sits all alone,
An eerie casted greyness;
Of every shade and tone.
Flicker again does the flame,
Caused by who knows what.... Ooh!
'If someone touched me now, I think I'd die of shock.
Sitting here with someone, we chat by its glow,
We laugh at its simplicity, just 'wax and string', you know.
Fascinated by the slowly melting wax,
The occasional escape as it filters through the cracks,
Forming those lumpy rivers as down the sides they chase,
To gather in a pool, to cool, rejected at its base.
Romantic luminosity, or simply light to see...
Always let your light shine that all around may see..
The love that's held; in God's serenity.
And then, when you light a candle,
Please....... Light it just for me.

## Magnific Trees

Misty hue, engulfing eerie silhouettes
Branches clattering, leaves all gone and yet
Grand and awesome standing,
Rugged, stark, forlorn,
Stripped of their former glory,
On this; a frosty morn.
No more to sway with breezes,
Which leaves like sails did know,
But chill wind passing through now
Ore boughs; abreast with snow.
Now dull, un'allureing are Summer's shady walks,
Where rustling, crisps noises and great oaks retort.
Until the Spring, when again there comes to each anew
A breath of life absorbing; then buds and leaves break through.
Endearing me to nature, my very soul to please,
Nothing ever quite the same,
As God's magnific trees.

## Une Rêvé Dancoise

Fred Astaire and Lionel Blaire, What a truly tireless pair.
Prancing shoes, tap and busy,
Their dancing makes me feel quite dizzy.
Dame Margot Fontaine, Such a glorious name,
Who hailed from Surrey's Reigate Town, (pronounced Tyne)
By a station on the Dorking line.
She could twirl and leap with such grace on her feet,
With which it would be hard to complete.

Now Rudolph Nureyev, with much more nerve than I have,
To parade around in those tights.
He could pirouette and arabesque the ladies to please;
With leaps to great heights, entangling his knees!
Speaking of which there's little Wayne Sleep,
Who truly springs… like he'd wings on his feet.
With Bonnie Langford, he made a great team..
I'm so glad she no longer, does sqweam and sqweam!
The actor Gene Kelly, who's reputations now a forgonna,
Then there's my favourite.. Donald O'Conner.
He danced with a doll, I laughed 'till in pain,
He sprang up the walls then down again.
Also resembled the late great Danny Kaye,
Who could sing, was so funny, oh! and he danced by the way.
But it's to 'Donald' I lift my proverbial cap,
And I dedicate these lines ole chap.
Darcy Bustle amazing star for times hence..
There's 'queen of contort', the great Louis Spence.
For of the many who danced on our silver screens,
Like Ginger and Adele, who were each Astaire's queens!
I can dance like them all,

(Effeminate voice) But, Only in my dreams.

## Nail Pierced

'Nail pierced hands;' they said,
And a spear in His side..
Thorns on His head
Then later He died.
No harm did He do… But,
More good than any other….
They let them crucify,
One, who unlike any other,
Would say He forgave them,
Then just glanced towards His Mother.

Nail pierced hands and feet,
I tremble at the thought
I shudder, as I imagine
His arms outstretched, taut.
Taking the weight of His body torn,
On that awful day..
Yet we mustn't mourn;
For such love as this
An example to us all;
'He' and 'His' truth lives on,
Soon will come 'His Dawn',
I await a 'King,'
Who's love lingers on….
'Father,' 'Son' and 'Holy Spirit,'
'Lord Jesus' **the only one**.

## Sunrise Sailing

The sound, the smell, the taste, the atmosphere
Sun rising and fresh, on a beach I hold so dear.
Light breeze and sail flaps, sheets pulled in tight,
Foresail bellows, then as she fills, mast and rigging retort.
So slowly at first, with great sense of expectancy,
Then, the first ripple as bow breaks thru' and sets you free.
Pull in the slack, adjust and settle down,
Throwing down the surplus sheet,
As you bring her 'steadily around.'

Then catching a glimpse as the shore slips slowly by,
Now gathering momentum, you heave a subconscious sigh.
Releasing all the tension, mind now on other things,
Cutting through the water, 'Oh! how my heart it sings.'
Then that special moment, as running with the wind,
Standing out on the gunwale, spray in face and find
That, along with the shore now, all stress left behind,
Lungs so full of freshness, the air as sweet as wine.

Out into the sunrise, to see what we shall find
Invigorating as the physical overpowers the mind,
Eventually to return but, not quite as before,
Tired, but body, mind and soul, demanding more and more.

**Sussex my Church**

On a Summer's evening, I take a walk to find
Answers to those questions, storming my mind.
Meander along the cliff path
As the sun is going down,
I take much solace in the peace,
With no one else around.
At one with the scenery
I begin to merge
And for 'A reason' I now
Begin to search.
Cliff top solitude, sunset evening time,
Gazing Westward at the sky,
It's colours quite sublime.
From this cliff top, seen clear across the bay,
Light now fading, at the end of this day.
My heart and mind,
As all  pressures of life
Slowly now….. unwind.

A Peace and tranquility
Not ever known before
Embraces and comforts me
I come to hurt no more.
Turning to absorb
This evening panorama,

Continued…….

Like the stage set of
Some grand melodrama;
I find I am now lifted and can plainly see,
The Earth and all its wonders down before me.
I sense there is a God
Far greater than any religion;
Wiser than all the ceremony,
Pomp and stiff tradition,
I find there is no reason now
To continue my search,
I realise that this spot right here
Could now become my church,
But this spiritual awareness
Is one that should be shared,
Built into the fabric
of society, layer by complex layer.

## Surprise rewards

December, my e mail got jammed;
Some virus got in… yet again.
So I had to phone my friend,
So good to hear their voice again.
Washing machine now leaking,
Got so behind with my chores..
Digging down deeper in my drawers,
Found a favourite, jumper that used to be yours.

'Power out,' so we sat in the dark,
We had to light a fire,
With some candles around.
Giving new views to admire.
We sat just chatting, then sang to my guitar,
I came to realise, **my home** is where **you** are.

We sat closer, listened harder,
Loved deeper, shared stories and song.
Came together more closely..
Began to feel that we belong.
Lost the keys to the car
With all our presents inside, so sad.
Stayed home with my family..
The best Christmas we ever had,
The best Christmas we ever, ever had.

Christmas 2012, a thought.

## Sleeping majority

What does it say of people who fight over petty things?
For pride or even borders
Which aren't seen or disappear.
No real boundary on the internet,
Their small minds endeavors
Bent on local news to tell.
Whilst creating for their children,
A world resembling hell.
Often fighting for the one single God,
The same by different names
Who their devotion, He must distain.
No part in this evil doing would God by proxy claim.
But like some ignorant children;
Fighting over an empty wrapper,
The contents standing, awesome, ignored to one side.
They claim rights to the package.
Absurd reasoning, in their lives
Failing to see the very content is the prize.
The world and so much 'Goodness',
Obscured by their lies.
This wonderful world, full of amazing diversity,
Beauty and so much to learn.
Most of its population can happily get along.
Work to clothe and feed each other,
Enabling each to become their best.
But less than 5% have power
To control and herd the rest,
Wake up silent majority,
We are being destroyed by
Our neglect and a minority.

## Misunderstood and accused

Never intending to do something wrong,
I find it most painful when accused;
Of something I just would not contemplate,
My intent misconstrued, this I really hate!
Never knowingly would I plan to mislead,
I don't set out to deceive!
Yet on occasion those who should know me well
Have introduced me to this kind of hell!
You said, " so and so!" they shout aloud!
That's not what was meant.. I then vowed!
How did this ever come to pass,
That you would judge me to the last;
On something which is far from how it was meant?
So much energy and effort is then spent!
When to know me as you really should,
It must be clearly understood!
I did not mean anything bad or intend
That which might bring about this end!
I have been affected immensely by your action
Against me in no small fraction…
Your response has been exaggerated and out of scale,
I have been accused of 'creating a tale!'
If you thought this of me, it is all so sad!
For my love for you is true and I'm glad.
I make no excuse for being who I am today;
I am so deeply sorry, 'Is all that I can say!'

11 – 01 - 2013

Elsie Robbins, 'nee Woodgate' centre 1928 with my Father on her lap.
Behind her is her Father Henry Elam Woodgate with his mother on his left and her mother Granny Ellis to our left. Rye's own local paper came and recorded the rare event of five generations. Henry made the stool!

My lovely Nan 'Elsie,' who I called on her birthday 1$^{st}$ January every year.

**Autumn**

Autumn has come,
We in the Summer of our lives,
Draw on our Springs the Winters to survive.
As the stream's dried bed
Begins its flow to swell,
Leaves drift and fluttering
Create their pungent spell.
Crisp, fresh is life, the senses all a tingle,
Drawn into solitude, so with peace to mingle.
Not to look back on things so dead and past.
But use the experiences
For things which love and last,
No effort or knowledge can make the leaves to stay,
Their time is over they have had their May.
Only 'Love' their their true beauty,
From this time hence.
We retain in our hearts, by way of remembrance.
So we welcome Autumn, not as a final end;
But as a new beginning which mere life transcends.
Not to mourn the passing of love we came to know,
But enhance in its memory;
All those springs we have yet to know.

For Dear NAN, Elsie Robbins. 1st Jan 1908 - 7 Oct 1990

Tulips in our fore court in Mayenne

## Blind Stupidity

Children playing in the garden
Happy sounds abound;
One is brown and his bright smile
Drawing other smiles around.
Beaming little faces
With no thought beyond their game,
Not even of who shall win;
To them it's all the same.
Innocent enjoyment, precious moments shared,
Their differences enhancing, only in fun compared.
But later, when as adults we take a look again,
What happened to this picture, when as grown men;
Change our outlook, learning prejudice,
Noticing colour, religion, type, even shape.
All that divides us and brings about such hate.
When we see a flower who can't appreciate;
Then seeing another, but different, we don't equate,
No one would say that all orange flowers are….
Better or worse, preferring one in particular.
They're all beyond our ability to change or alter.
We accept them, so why not our sons and daughters.
Their differences enhancing, so open your eyes,
Division is the devils work, I would surmise.
What is it that we learn in growing older?
That brings about this awful change,
Our hearts; then growing colder.
Ignore appearances, but see the love instead,
Finding mutual purpose then cut away a head.

## Love on Loan

I had a dream when our little boy did die,
Of arms outstretched, reaching down, from the sky.
Embracing, receiving, reclaiming the love,
That had only been lent by the power above.
Shortcutting all the mischief and decay,
The slow evolving into a 'Man of today.'
But simply enhancing our days for a while,
Generating 'kicks' and our beaming smiles.
Then just before the world could taint his little soul,
He returned to the Father we shall all come to know.
We're better for knowing him, even though now apart,
This little boy is held within our hearts.

Love as pure as God's never wants you to suffer,
He now looks down on this Father and Mother.
I dreamed, whilst he shared their suffering and pain,
He longed for them to be happy and laugh again,
Not to be associated with any anger and hurt,
But rather see celebration at his birth.
Their times together, in memory retain.
Until 'all,' with the Father, are together again.

December 1978.

For Jonathan our son, born Nov 5th 1977

**The Invitation**

Praise be to God the universe creator,
Greater than all religion, any being or kirk.
Whom nothing will confine, restrict or alter.
Division a weakness, can be the devils work

.

One Almighty God, Lord over all,
Accessible to us only through Grace,
Will you accept now as Saviour, Jesus?
As Lord and Master, who died in your place.

Paying for your sins and all transgressions,
Sent by God a true gift from above.
Who now in Spirit is right here amongst us,
Waiting for you to embrace His love.

Knock on the door you've been invited,
There is no secret, let me show you how.
Call on His name, kneel now before Him,
Feel His Holy presence embrace you right now.

Allow all the hurt, dissolution and pain
Like dirty rags with all sin we distain,
Be washed away by the blood of the Lamb,
Spilt on that Calvary hill, so we claim.

Continued……

For all fall short of the glory that's God's.
That at least is quite plain to see,
Only through Jesus may we come before God,
As cleansed and as righteous as we need to be.

So accept Jesus now, as your Lord over all,
Then die to yourself and answer His call.
This invitation comes now to you direct,
By Spirit, through Jesus, from God,
With **immediate effect**.

**It is my sincerest desire that my family, friends and all who read this would study this poem twice; Then read it aloud with 'gusto!'**

**Phillip Robbins.**

**Woman**

Oh! Such perfection, sweet Heaven on Earth!
Praise and thanks to the power
That brought about the birth-
The creation of magnificent splendor in form,
Beauty and elegance, as fresh as a Summer's morn.

Desirable, with a complexion
Like that of a fresh ripe peach;
Round, full, vivacious,
Firm, yet soft are each.
Curves so inspiring
To an artist's careful eye-
Warm, tender, smooth
A far better subject than any sea or sky.

How brilliant! How clever!
To have as a vision in soul and mind
And then, even better, to go on and find
The idea, a dream that could be made so real.
The ability to create what I have come to feel
Is the epitome of success
As the ultimate designer,
For none and no other will ever do it finer,
To bring into being
The most perfect form known to man,
There back in Eden's garden, where it all began.

Continued……

Man, who came first, is a wonder to perceive
But was shadowed, on the second round,
When introducing Eve.
Not in any sojourn, not anywhere in space,
Is perfection so complete
As woman's body soul and face.

( Additional verse.. Only for comic effect.
Not intended to give offence!)

What a pity to then go on and to find,
Nothing can be done to understand her mind.

Previously published in.
**Woman**, an Aural Images Anthology
Edited by Susan White 1996
ISBN No: 0 9521677 6 X

**Autumnal Disarray 1992**

Radiant shafts a'streaming,
Enhanced by sunlight through trees down a leafy lane,
Winding through this England; which shall be great again.
Mossed, dank and cool, where in Summers past,
Leaves in multitude of splendor;
Now fade then die at last.
Bringing such colour as we,
Could not with mere words describe,
Without enhanced by that Spirit
By which we shall survive.
Walking with these notions
Attuned and now as one,
Each moment is appreciated,
But when all is quite done,
Any vague recollection
Will do anything to enhance,
What may be achieved in..
One enlightening glance.

Ambered splendor dazzling
With shades of brown between,
Reds also apparent,
Punctuate with some evergreen.
Vibrant, contrasting colours,
Which no artists pallet ever made,
Nor ever so very splendid..
Could man, thus be arrayed.

Continued.........

Shaped and sculpted by
Their type or situation
Against the bluest sky,
They sway in animation.
Along the hedgerows laying,
Now just cast away,
A rust and amber carpet
In Autumnal disarray.

Proud, but ever humbled,
Remembering so many who have died,
In keeping this our England free,
This our wondrous countryside.
So now for God and Queen
We must strive to serve,
May every man and boy
His rewards deserve,
Then each and every woman
In this land we call our home
Rise and stand together,
Our 'tempered steel' to hone.
That which made us great,
Shall make us great again.
Take a good look around you
From all despair refrain.
Take stock of your inheritance,
This land of history,
Of justice and Magna Carta,
Where both rich and poor be free.

Continued..............

Let everyone be proud of
What has gone before, but
Plan now for the future,
With all it has in store.
Thinking of our children
Who must follow in our wake,
Educate them  to take the reins,
For this Kingdom's sake.

After the Autumn, comes again
That wondrous gift that's Spring,
Then leaves will again embrace those trees,
Again the birds shall sing.
God is up in Heaven;
We, His realm do roam,
Keep 'Him' in your soul,
Your heart to be His throne.
Inspiring and rewarding for
Those who would turn to see,
Let it warm and encourage you,
That this; shall forever be.
03-11-92

( Sent to Prince Charles.. Reply came via an Equerry. )
"His royal Highness; appreciates the sentiments of your enclosure…"

**Awaiting Adolescence**

Little boy walking along a sea shore,
For what are you seeking?
Just what are you looking for?
In dreams, he sees them, standing very tall.
In a harbour somewhere by an old sea wall.
Bobbing, gently waiting
The light of early dawn,
When the tide now out; its duty will perform.
Gentle breezes bringing a perfect day.
Not long now to wait,
Until cutting through the foam,
Out to sea, tall ships, his soul with them.
Where his spirit can freely roam.

Out across the oceans all around the globe,
To lands and places way beyond any he can know,
Even as he stands there his feet upon the shore;
The tall ships now leaving, you can't ignore
This small boy waving frantically
As they cut across the bay. Sending you his best wishes,
As he'll watch you sail away,
He prays that he might come with you,
When '**adolescence**' he has found.
For he's told that it's something
That in His present youth he needs,
That he too might sail away,
Across those seven seas

. 11-08-84

## A beacon

Let us be a light, a beacon in this land.
For those who are lost,
That they might understand.
A path is there just waiting
To a gate 'open wide',
The journey will be much easier
With Lord Jesus at your side.
Show us dear Lord your purpose,
Use us day by day
That we may better serve you,
Our sins all washed away.
No other who has died
Was worthy of the price,
Or could ever pay this debt,
By forfeiting their life.
God so loved the world,
Also His children all there in,
Despite all their transgressions
Their indifference and sin.
God, knowing us better than we can ever know ourselves,
Gave us the one thing, He loved above all else.
His own dear Son Jesus,
Who now reigns above
As master of all Heaven,
King of all in love!

Continued…..

Precious in all eyes
That would only turn to see,
The Saviour of our very Souls
Yes;  especially you and me.
So praise His Holy name together,
Go out and spread this news,
That Jesus is the answer,
So please don't refuse
The peace and love that's given
In His precious name,
With this small spark in greeting,
Light a mighty flame.

Go now and tell your friends,
Neighbours and family too.
How else shall they all learn,
If it doesn't come from you?
Be a witness of this truth,
Love and peace may then surely come,
When all as one body in God's church…

….**shall march on.**

19 – 11 - 94

The ferry going home to France was always emotive.

In 2008 we moved back to Sussex and family.
We were so privileged to have had those 5 years in Mayenne, but the best days were always when friends and family came and shared it with us.

## On Balance

My friends I just have tell you,
As it seems only fair,
Even though it may surprise you
I simply have to share
The news which has been burning in my heart
But first I must warn you from the very start,
That only because I value your friendship so very true,
I risk your displeasure, when I bring to you.
The fact that I believe in Jesus, and do intend!
That you too shall know Him, before your final end.

Because in 'life after death,' I feel what is said is true,
So when I go to Heaven, I hope to be with you.
So when we're looking down upon our lives then past,
You'll be so very glad you'd a friend who until the last.
Shared the very greatest thing, that he had to give.
The knowledge that thanks to God,
After death, you too can live.
With the knowing that all debts are paid in full,
By someone who could afford the bill.
The Saviour of us all, He's your ticket up to Heaven
Don't fight it or give me grief,
For to see you understand this
Would bring me such relief.
To know then, that when I go to Heaven,
To be with God above.
All around I will find those friends I've come to love.
15 – 09 – 92

## Dreams please

At the end of almost every day
I endeavor to unwind
Just before I go to sleep
I almost never find
A single thing to distract,
My mind so ill at ease.
So eager to continue,
To tantalize and tease.

Words forever pounding
Like those shouted at an auction,
Should these rhymes written down
Be tools to, earn my fortune
I would gladly write all night, yet I have a notion,
That tomorrow, too tired to wake,
I'll be last for a promotion.

So let me sleep, quickly I say.
Please, please words just go away.
Let me rest my weary head;
Sink down into my soft warm bed.
So now to slumber on this night,
Not know ought 'till morning light.
All can be ok, oh! So right,
I'll stretch and yawn,
Then to say....     "Good night!"

06 – 08 – 84

.

Our daughter Sarah; as with our lovely boys Matt and Jamie are the blessings which are such undeniable evidence' in our lives, of the presence of our faithful Father God. Such as these wonderful people; cannot be only of our doing. Greater forces than mere humanity must at work.

Thank you Lord and Amen

**Blessed by heaven**

Born of precious moments,
How can mere man perceive
The true value, the magnitude
Of how life is conceived?
Out of love and passion,
Into the world we shall know.
A gift blessed by heaven, from a seed we now sow.
To start from such small beginnings into a child to grow,
A life we shall share, encourage, love and support.
Scold when they are naughty, or
At least when they are caught.

But right now, this moment content to contemplate,
The wonder of life itself and what's to come quite soon.
When you feel gentle lumps and bumps
Manipulate the womb.
Then that panic disarray when at last that special day.
The time has come to dash about,
Those pre packed bags, you jump and shout.
When it's your first time, it's such a fright,
Yet there is time, it could take all night.
So rest as ease for when all calms,
The reality is a baby in your arms,
So great an experience that most will say,
"On bended knees, I thankfully pray!"

08 – 08 – 84
For our; Sarah, Marie – Louise 26 - 10 – 1984

## Eternal maze

Sometimes when we lose a friend,
It's tempting to imagine, 'This is the end.'
No more the pleasant, friendly chat,
Baring our souls on this and that.
Precious moments, so very hard to find,
Which will stay forever in one's mind.
A special smile, a gesture….
Perhaps some turn of phrase,
Now all gone forever,
Into life's eternal maze.

Unless we weave the threads
Of those memories so sweet and true,
Into the fabric of our days,
This to enhance their colours hue.
Brightening and shining on those days,
We have yet to know,
The memories of a good friend,
In the seeds their life did sow.

For Jacky April 1990

## Global suicide

Every morning the sun shines
Way up in the skies,
Even when the clouds obscure it from our eyes.
Every day the the oceans wash our very shores,
Unaware of the seasons or what they have in store.
Reliable, relentless, the plants and trees they grow,
Despite our intervention, beyond all we know.

We ignore such beauty,
Caught in our selfishness.
Blind often to this perfection,
Indulging in our awful mess.
Tearing down forests faster than they grow,
Polluting the pastures where seed we should sow.
Poisoning the waters, defiling all creation,
Caretakers of the very planet.... or
Destroyers of our nation.

When shall we learn? from behind this farce we hide,
Allowing this murder,
This '**global suicide**'.

1988

**Don't hold back**

The Lord has a purpose for each, one and all.
So when you hear His invite, answer His call.
You never really doubted,
Your vision has just been clouded.
But, you've nothing to lose, so give it your all.
Take some time alone, take stock of life and things.
Look around, beyond the immediate,
The despair that this often brings.

You owe it to yourself, to see the face of God,
If you want to know the truth, then give a little nod.
Because if it's all true then great!
Jump in, don't hold back.
Where are you going to fall to?
Things really aren't so very black.
If they are, you will remain all alone,
If nothing is really there; so what is; or can be lost?
Perhaps only your despair.

But what if it's all true? That there's more to your life.
You may have been missing out, swamped in trivial strife.
Just the knowing that your worth the saving,
Christ's blood can set you free,
Then let Him have died for a reason,
Yes even you and me.
When accepting this, **If you understand**,
On your knees cry out….
Lord Jesus, please take me as I am.

14 – 04 - 94

## Our Shepherd ( Farmer's accent! )

Some say the Lord is our shepherd;
Now this I can't dispute.
But some days I feel that He needs a longer crook.
For them that gets away, the doers of 'naughty deeds.'
Them that's loud and bad, sowers of naught but weeds.

But then again there's freedom,
To do as we bloomin' like.
You don't have to crawl
On your knees in prayer each night.

He caught me right enough and
I was dodging real fast,
Well, His crook must be long enough,
**Considering my past!**

Before in a crowd, I was all alone with no true friend to call,
Well! None I trust in times of real need, no hopers one and all.
Whatever He saw in me, at the time I wasn't fussed,
But now, I've friends a plenty and ones I can trust.

So to me it really matters now, all that I say and do.
Because to Him; I should pay a debt that is so very true.
Yet only Grace can save me, there's no action I could ever do.
Jesus died and paid the price for the likes of me and you.
So people must see in 'me,' some substantial change,
Because in all I do, I'll try, to glorify His precious name.

13 – 09 – 89

## Phillip

At my baptism by the reverend Oscar E Brookes,
In Rye my home town in God's holy presence.
They said to all around this boy shall be called
Phillip Anthony Robbins and so ever since,
I endeavor to keep the given name
Not Phil or any other which I came to disdain.
Having spent some forty years telling folk to refrain.
Working abroad and often called Philippo Antonio
I quite liked this as it sounded like a Romeo.
In France Phillippe Antoine for two seasons was such fun
But when back in England, that's where trouble began.
So if you wouldn't mind, as a follower of Christ,
I much prefer the name I was given for life.
God was present, also many of His Angels,
I feel that when I go to heaven there at last I will;
Be called by the name I was given at my birth.
Not some truncated abbreviation,
Like down here on Earth.

03 – 01 – 94

My sketch of Rye church where I was christened 1953

Taken on holiday in St Tropez 2012; with Anna, Sarah, Danny Ruby, Grace and our Jamie. We had an air conditioned luxury chalet on the beach. In June just after my 59th birthday. Anna's was on 18th June there,.

Only 10 minutes from Sarah and Danny' with the girls and Jamie, who all came to us every day for 10 of the 17 days we spent down there. So different from those 17 other trips down to the area since 1994. When we stayed in our caravan on the same pitch 1 allee le Draio next door.

**Taller horizons**

We can pray for world peace,
But, your will be done.
If your returning; requires this course to run.
Then let it be as you have planned,
The solution is different from where we stand!
We have prayed for a cure for all our ills and pains,
Not always thanking you for our many recent gains.
Only **your Love** could forgive these sins,
Let us trust you more in all and everything!
Our perspective is clouded,
Our reasoning misguided,
There is one who would lead us astray!
Confuse and exaggerate and so leading us away,
Off the path from which we should never strayed!
So help us concede to your will
To listen when we all pray.
Refreshing our relationship with you,
Each and every day!

03 – 09 – 1996

A CHRISTIAN
BED TIME STORY

# MISSING YOU

(C)

BY
PHILLIP A ROBBINS

Filanpine Press and Publishing 2013

**Missing you**

In a dream. I was preparing for a ride into the sky,
Graceful, quiet, gliding, soaring way up high.
To views and other things which could not be described,
In a hot air balloon, with all my friends inside.

But just before we could depart
I felt an aching in my heart.
For one could not come, he had to alight before the start.
It seems he had no ticket, no membership you see…
Not like my loved ones, my family and me.

As nice as he was and with plenty of room aboard,
He was left behind as we all to Heaven soared.

Don't be left behind, my dream it seemed to say.
But take stock right now, before 'judgment day.'
Don't put off my friends what you must know is true,
Because you'll miss out on what's waiting there for you.

The fare's already paid, you only claim the ticket.
If you don't before you die, its stay behind and like it.

So when I reach heaven, for I'm not missing this show,
I really want around me
All those friends I have come to know.

**Don't be left behind**
**My dream, it seemed to say.**
**But take stock right now**
**before that judgement day.**

**to see you claim your ticket,**
**with all that you can gain,**
**to see you accept this truth,**
**is my sincerest aim.**

**So, when I am a pain**
**It just to let you see;**
**That even if you**
**don't decide....**
**You know where I will be.**

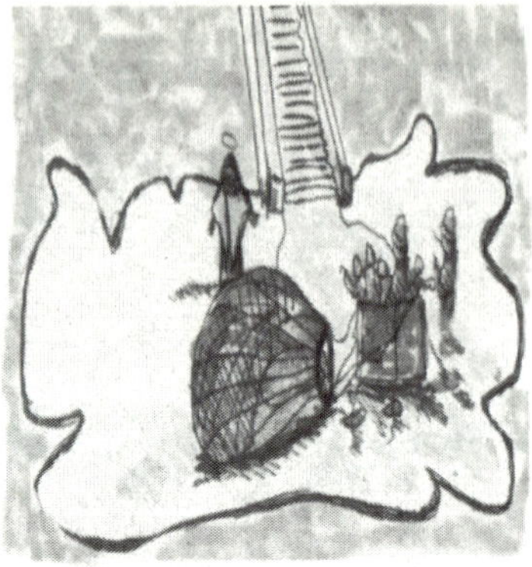

**Just admit that you're less,**
**Than God would have you be,**
**Accept that His grace only**
**Can really set you free.**

08 – 09 – 92

Now an illustrated Children's book. On Lulu.com

Order copies for your friends at robbinsrest@sky.com
Or call us on **00 44 (0) 793 114 9304**

**Filanpine Press and Publishing 2013**

## Precious Time

There is a precious time which comes every year;
When people come together; to share times of cheer.
When it is acceptable to greet a stranger met
Without all the falsehood, when presents we give and get.
Time spent at home sat by a fire, setting one's hopes on…
Matters intellectually higher.

The radio bringing  comfort and spice,
News and entertainment, to oil the wheels of life.
This very precious time when families exchange
Tokens of their love.
Bringing them closer to the will of God above.
His plans we ignore; other weeks of the year,

This precious time is 'Christmas' with sentiments sincere.
I fear that **God's plan** may often come to naught,
Few seeing beyond those gifts received and bought.
Becoming hardened to aspects; which should bring pride to man.
Content often to ignore all this, seeming not to understand.

So, if you get my meaning and agree with what I say,
Please spread this 'precious time' beyond just Christmas day.
Particularly for those children..
Who's future depends on 'us' today….

21 – 12 - 93

I had the honour to be 'Santa' at our Ruby's first school Christmas bazaar in 2012. Ruby as my assistant fairy did not want her school chums to know I was not the real Santa. Over 70 children in about 3 hours.. Phew!

Our sons Matthew on the right with Jamie in 1996

**Such blessings are these two special young men to us.**

## Our Boys

A son is a likeness, so like oneself and yet!
An individual being with a mind of his own; you bet!
For his smile and cheek, any faults in him you seek;
Blame them on his Mother, include that stubborn streak!
Of course all the good things; when clever and doing fine,
Then I can tell you that he's mine, all mine!
Yet that certain something in the way that he smiles,
When kindness and gentleness; with energy beguiles.
He can remind me of Her when oh so very young;
Camped out in moon light, sang our favourite song.
So much a part of us, of that there is no doubt.
Even when displeased; that impish little pout,
As gradually though the years this cheeky little elf,
Has taken from us all and grown up into himself.

For Matthew and Jamie. September 1984

**Precious Things**

Often life comes in chapters
Of unpredictable events,
One finds oneself confused
By all that it presents.
Then it's time to take stock,
Of all that you have achieved.
List all that's good; then disregard what you don't need.

Focusing on the good that's gone,
Bring it to the fore, then boldly move right on.
Dust off all the sadness, recalling all that's fine,
Claiming all that's wholesome tell yourself 'that's mine!'

Building upon these special things
Keeping them all 'close too,'
For they shall sustain; bringing comfort to you.
So never regret what has been and is now gone,
Both the good and the bad times;
Providing the strength required to carry on.

In memorandum of a full and valued life. 01 – 11 - 93

Written for the dear mother of 'Daniel' a guitarist friend.

## Perpetual stream

Stream; ever flowing, running, gurgling, rippling onwards.
Always winding and twisting as and where they should.
As only God knows how or why…
Reflecting both cloud and sky.
Around a bend, beneath a bough of willow stooped;
Then even further now.
Ever onward, for ever more, 'till at last at oceans door,
To clash, then mingle with salty shore.
Beneath your silvery sheen does flow
All your treasures, yet I know;
Weathered both in wind and storm,
You'll wend on forever on and on.
Over Summer's sun scorched pebbles,
Under bridges where it echo's.
From banks along the way you take,
All, 'flotsam and jetsam' in your wake.
Yet, in Winter's harsh array;
Beneath the ice, still you may.
Be seen to wander on at will,
Never, not ever, to be still.
Through lock and weir, falls and shallow,
Even where the coarse be narrow.
Bubbling, pooled before a dam or out into a pond,
Somewhere, somehow on you flow
Through towns then on beyond.

**Proud Fool**

I am proud to be Christian;
I've come to know it's all true,
But some folks are so stubborn
I don't mind telling you.
Someone asked me, "Why do you believe?"
"In someone called Jesus?"
They think I am naive!
You've never really seen Him
It's all only hearsay,
What's all this nonsense about
'Our debts He's paid?

I felt a fool just then,
I couldn't find the words,
When I tried to explain
I looked the more absurd.
They said,
"Wasn't He some baby; born in a stable?"
Or "I think that's the fable…!"
"It's all just religion, for weak folk with doubts!"
"They need something to cling to..!"
"With all those 'thee's and thou's.!"

Continued…………..

Then in a flash I said;
"Now just suppose that God,
Could only reach down; to those religious 'clods'!"
"Only Bishops and church goers,
The supposed devout and true."
"But then; just suppose; he only wanted
To come and be with you!"

He knows you would just flip
If He arrived at your door,
So He sent a little baby, need I say much more…?

The Son of man, to lead a generation.
Now others follow on from nation to nation.
He brought God down to Earth,
Right to our very feet.
Rolling out the ' **red carpet** '
To each door on your street.
If you will accept 'This invite,'
To walk at His side,
I know that you too would find reason..
To Boast, **LORD JESUS** with pride.

27 October 1992

## Reign in awe

Woodland path meander
Along twist and bend today,
Between your flowered carpets,
Which no mere mortal lay.
Meander on and down into,
The forest's deeper heart;
Passing the busy wildlife
Of 'breeze and bird' to hark.

Primrose and fresh daffodil
Bracken and forget-me-not,
Then into a clearing
This quiet, hallowed spot.

Peaceful, gently scented
To dream all alone,
In these realms of glory
A tree stump; for a throne.

Then later to return
Along these paths of wonder to roam,
Leaving trees and every creature
The sanctity of their 'awesome home.'

12 – 04 – 91

## Mirrors of your Love

Make of a well Lord; filled with holy water,
That those we meet might drink
Their lives so then to alter.
That they thirst for your Spirit, hunger for your love,
Then seek for that guidance which comes from above.

Make of us an instrument; playing in your band,
Use us in Your music, to achieve this day; Your plan.
Guide us to your glory , use us to achieve,
Peace, love and understanding
As and where there is need.

Make of us a tool Lord, use us all at work,
Let us not this day our duty to You shirk.
But, lead us from doing;
Those things which hurt and maim,
Help us through 'Your power Lord'
To glorify Your Name.

Make us all mirror's; of 'Your Love'
Channels for your spirit, leaders amongst people
With your Love we can do it.
That through 'You' we can show
Each corner of this nation
A glimpse of 'Your Love'
Open the path to salvation.

15 – 10 – 90 20th century Psalm awaiting a tune.

**Ignorant market** (A folk song)

London is glistening in the rain;
People shopping; foods to gain.
As they hurry on their way,
Desperately trying to pass their day.

'Fresh today,' marketeers cry…
No one listens, I wonder why?
The hustle, bustle in the streets,
The perpetual scuffle of busy feet.

Further down a small boy cries,
He sobs for his mother, tear stained eyes.
'Me' shoppin's heavy!' one wife nags,
Ordering her hubby, ''Take these bags!'

The market's clatter and busy noise,
Loud men in hats selling funny toys.
Shouting 'Luv'ly matas for next to nowt!'
'Come and get your greens and sprouts!'

The rain has stopped, a rainbow appears,
Glowing in the drenched dank atmosphere,
The blues, red and yellows fall,
No one stops to look at all.

Inspired by a shorter poem,
by my Brother Stephen Robbins 1969

**Silent awe** (Spiritual moments) . 02 – 12 - 93

Looking out to sea
On a late summer's eve
The waves gently
Lapping in the
Westerly breeze.
Up high on these cliffs where the views are best,
I'm gazing out to sea turning my eyes to the West.
As the sun is setting on Dorset's sleeping shores.
I don't need religion to stand in silent awe,
Whilst standing here
I sense… I know
That there is
Something more..
More than
Just sea and sky.
This news I can't ignore,
I've become aware that God
Who is Greater
Than any one faith,
With Christ more central
As I find a path to Glory;
These Spiritual moments;
On a hill by the sea holds more in witness
Than any mere story.
Because out here I'm further
From all the pain and hurt,
Feeling more at peace right now;
So this shall be my church.

## Sold out

Pathetic is the word which springs to my mind,
When I think of the pretensions; of an 'arrogant mankind'.
With God given ingenuity, a row of 'lit street lights,'
Illuminates only briefly to guide us home each night.

The knowledge to create all the power for this deed,
The coal to light those furnaces
Bringing warmth where there's need.
With the genius to design the means to generate,
Electricity for these lights; I agree the achievement's great.

But, not to be compared to the sun as an alternative at night,
To think, that any problem, man could make it right.
Then return in a thousand years
When all fuel has burned away,
Gone with all those species we've killed or worse, I say….

For, with all his ingenuity, cleverness and spark!
When the lights go out and man leaves us in the dark,
Exactly how does he respond to this sincere remark?
How then please tell me? will he begin a new start?,

12;20 am 05 – 10 – 93

One of my personal, favourite poems. It expresses clearly the desperate anxiety I felt that night after seeing some fool saying global warming was a passing natural event, not at all caused by any activity by the human race. Surely, we should be 'on this' and 'all over it.' If stopping tree cutting and reducing smoke and pollution can help the ozone to mend, why are we not all 'demanding action'. NOW!

<u>Our detached lack of action is truly pathetic.</u>

Phillip A Robbins 19 – 12 – 2012

## Song thrush

Handsome song thrush waiting perched on lichened wall,
By the fern and hedges,   whilst leaves, around you fall.
From the warmth I watch you as you flick and preen,
Out in the Winter garden, only the evergreen;
Brings warmth and splendor, all else brings only change.
Slowly the pretty garden it's colours to rearrange,
Seasons changing colours bearing branch and bough,
Views of other parts, no leaves obstructing now;
Ever changing viewpoints like seasons here and gone.
The Autumn song bird observes, enhancing all with song.
Other birds around him; a Robin joins their praise,
Of all things unexplainable, we'll value all our days.
Now handsome songster gone and soared into the blue,
Just up and left us pining; flown to pastures anew.
He up and left us the richer, if we'd just turn to see,
We should appreciate such glory, which is forever free.

03 – 12 – 92
Written whilst visiting an Ardingly, care home,.

**Street cred**

He asked, "Do you believe in Jesus?"
I said, "No way Jose,"
"I'm sure He lived long ago!
But who is He today?"
"It's not my scene. I'll lose my street cred!"
"I'm a '**Now type person**,
Get that into your head!"

Cool cats don't dig Jesus It's square and all that jazz,
It's not good for my image,
What do you mean… "That's sad!"
We're all quite happy just one day at a time.
We don't know where we're going..
But were getting there,  just fine.

Now my mates are gone..   please tell me more,
I'll hear what you have to say,
but leave any decisions
**For another day…..**

**April 1990**

## Sophie

Feeling despondent? Dejected and low?
The world and all its problems
Have dulled your inner glow?
Sunken are your shoulders,
Eyes turned towards the ground?
Wandering aimlessly? Not seeing what is around?

Raise your eyes dear child, focus up ahead!
Breath deep of the air, clear all doubt from your head.
Note all those colours, the vastness and beauty seen,
Just sense the majesty, count those shades of green.

Let it comfort and encourage you
That all that is near and far,
From way beyond these horizons;
The Lord's right where you are.

So precious to Him; that His Son came down to die,
Paying the price for everyone….
Yes, even you and I!
So raise your head dear child, ( Sophie )
Walk further down the path,
Focus on the Master, for when it comes to pass!
That standing then before Him
Later fully grown,
Your soul may then reap;
What this day your mind has sewn..

For little Sophie Bassett 18 – 12 – 93

## 'Starlite' nights (Our Band in the 80s)

At first there is a silence, the seats look quite forlorn
The daylight seems to invade, until with curtains drawn.
Then with gentle spot lighting, atmosphere to create
The clink of glass and bottle, shelves stocked for clients sake.

The rattle of the handle… "Someone get the key!"
"That must be the band,!" " there's usually just the three!"
Through the doors we filter, bringing all our gear.
Drums, keyboards, guitar and P/A
So the ones at the back can hear!

Then as together the pieces slowly fit,
Each item to its place; there seems no end to it.
So finally the last lead plugged into place;
We do a 'sound check' of 'feedback' there is no trace!
Now pleased with the amplifier's welcome 'thump!'
As the sound from mic, through lead, to speaker's jump!'

Gradually filling the seating around about,
"Get your raffle tickets!" someone shouted out.
Then with a drink in hand, we turn to face our gear.
Apprehension tingles as the moment draws closer near.

"We'll start with a quick step!" one of us will say.
So with this decision, our band begins to play.
Crowds of dancing people cover the chalked wood floor,
Foxtrots, waltzes, country and pops, they dance and ask for more.

Continued…..

So on to later, the raffle and a welcome break!
Before, 'back again' we're playing a mood to create.
More waltzes, disco a samba even some rock-n-roll!
Twisting, jive and smooches we sing and play them all.

Sing-a-long to Latin, we continue to mix the styles
We know they are all happy,
By the beaming friendly smiles.
All too soon it's ended; we play 'God save the Queen!'
For most British legions, will know what this shall mean!
Time to drink up the remainder of the beer
Put on their coats, go home, but we must linger hear.
To put away our things, the guitars, P/A and mike's
Pack up all the leads and gear for other '**Starlite nights**.'

For over 7 years we played so many gigs and venues of all kinds. The camaraderie and experience some of the best of my fondest of memories. We did not play together for over 12 years, being solo acts, but then for one afternoon reformed at a 'marquee' bar for the Queens Jubilee celebrations for fun. It was as though we had never stopped, immediately we were back in 'harness' and able to play a three hour set.

## Temporary Profits

All man has done is prove that he is blind,
To anything that really matters, time after time.
The gadgets and comforts that he can create;
Bringing about such greed, hunger and hate.
All 'man' has done could be wiped clean away,
Much never missed, yet still! 'His' debt we're left to pay!

For the fouling of our waters, the defiling of our air,
For squeezing out the last, he has a certain flair!
Gaining temporary profit at a greater, later cost;
By using up facilities which then are forever lost.

Not just to feed the hungry!
Or sustain our meagre girth,
But wanton destruction,
Exchange gimmicks for our Earth.
"Not a fair swap!" I hear you mournfully cry!
Well, do nothing about it; like the rest you'll die!

Take a look around you.
Think what has come to pass!
Would anything remain if unattended to the last?
To withstand the elements and nature taking over?
Given time all 'Man' has achieved,
Will simply be no longer!

The points quite clear.
You should not need this reminder!
The world and all that's in it.
Had a far better designer.
Nothing 'Man' has done
Could stand the true test of time,
All that is 'natural' can reclaim and then refine.

Continued……

Growing even through concrete,
Restoring from seed,
Reproducing and so glorifying
With ample for our needs.
So share the profits and show more respect;
Planning to work 'with' nature,
Then overcome neglect.
Let common sense be governor
Of how we harvest our world,
Please, let the flag of true wisdom,
Be then properly unfurled.

August 1993

**The few and you**

Life is a special gift, a short span of time,
When enhanced with health and happiness;
With many friends in line.
Can be taken for granted, it's preciousness obscured!
We can then lose sight of values, with vital rules ignored!

Forgetting the **air** free for us to breathe,
The awesome wonder of plants; grown from tiny seed.
The adventure of feasting ones eyes on mountains high.
Sunsets over the water, reflecting a wondrous sky!

Birds that sing, those creatures both small and great,
People of every colour, culture, character and shape.
All this is the 'real' thing, without 'Man's' design or plan,
It would continue unaided with infinite span…..

But for the few, who like maggots; infest what is pure!
Like termites in a priceless chest or some oaken furniture,
What is worse than **that** is whilst knowing, 'all's not right!'
Still we are not even halting,
We should be correcting… both day and night!

Stopping the rot, purifying our priceless water,
When will we stop defiling, our habit's then to alter?
Those few who bring injustice
In their vile, murderous raids,
The cost of rebuilding alone could fund a cure for 'aids!'

Continued…..

What is worse; is watching
These 'Few' who hurt and maim ,
Defile our tomorrow's and all we should disdain..
They kill little children, our wives and take the future..
Of those 'who not yet born,' will be too late to alter.
Much worse is the knowing and still blaming these few…
Whist ignoring the fact, solutions, begin with you!

28 – 11 – 93

**Waters meet in** Devon. Inspired many poems and became the cover of my first book of poems in 1996. Took photo with box camera 120.

Last photo on real just turned and snapped to finish the film. Only when developed did I see what I had taken. Down into dark, up into light!

**Waters meet**

Here this holy April a deep and green ravine,
Lost in flowered sides,
I lose pride and conceit.
Cool, green, fresh with sunshine might describe,
Yet somehow this and all description is incomplete.

For scent of the Spring flowers,
The mosses and wet stone.
The sounds of running water,
Where path through rock has hewn.

An atmosphere with which no words will suffice,
To adequately capture; what is now before our eyes.
Tree lined and deep in fragrant sunlight steep
Here in Lynton Devon…
In this sweet, waters meet.

12 – 04 – 91 Inspirational place in Devon.

## Welcome end

When in contemplation of one's final demise,
I found myself indulging in what came as a surprise.
A vision of classless closeness I sensed;
Such a wholesome peace and support,
The wonderful embracing.. Creeds of every sort.
Reaching out to welcome, comfort, sooth and love,
In a universe of 'well-being' suspended above.
Then in another world not physical or material,
Yet, more real, than any other.
Whilst beyond most men's dreams;
A vision of peacefulness all anxiety falls away,
Relief through forgiveness,
From all ill's and pains it seems,
Your **'Inner spirit'** soars as the body falls to decay.
No more to be supressed, but free to fly
Now gone, with all fear and dismay.
As outward and upward, expanding…
Stretched; so again, to meet.
The Father and home, from which it came,
No more mortal restraints to….
From your home, you keep!

24 – 04 - 93

## Yet I see Him

For some there is no God and Jesus who was dead,
Cannot be alive again.. no way! no how! They've said.
Yet I have seen Him, He walks with me some days.
He shows Himself to me in so many different ways.
In children and faces I see often on my way,
But! I couldn't see Him here, in town today!
Pushing and shoving, violence and crime,
Unhappy; so many are mean and unkind.
Then I thought I caught a glimpse when
The Sun came out for a while.
Some people stopped and stared,
Some even cracked a smile,
But all too soon distracted, back again to what they were,
A pity, but the fact is they really are absurd!
To cause each other pain and bring about this woe
When there is a truth and warmth for them,
In one they're just afraid to know!

April 1990

**Another night photo taken at our farm in Mayenne.**

The views and wonderful skies screaming the glory of God so loudly, most guests commented on how they unwound and became relaxed and many said they sensed a 'quiet,' commenting on the awesome views and night skies.

## Horse

Elegant, reliant powerful with grace;
Whether harnessed to a plough,
Or out on a steeple chase.
The ever loved and revered,
Always admired yet often even feared.

Useful, playful friend of man,
Trained for many varied deeds.
Towing great barges, pulling carts,
As and wherever they fit the needs.
I would love to ride away,
Gallop o're hedge and gorse!
The frisky stallion, mare in foal;
My Kingdom for a horse!

Whether wooden rocking toy,
Or snorting, stabled beast.
Everyone should love to own;
Or hire at the very least!
Even for just one hour
On a sunny afternoon,
So experience for yourself the fun,
That is forever 'Horse and groom!'

Summer 1984

**Growing love**

I recall as a youngster, a cub scout so new,
Sunday bible class, with doubts so very few.
I was introduced to a man who in the end,
Became the very dearest companion,
Both a saviour and a friend!

Drawn by His compassion, I came to know His word.
I loved Him then, but could not have told the world!
Through the years, my mind;
Often on other things, career, job and friends.
With the pressures they all bring.
But when I turned to look; back where I was before,
This man had never left me, I loved Him even more.

Asking Him to enter my life,  Intent to change the world!
Righteous armour gleaming
I wielded the word like a sword.
Frightening away some dear folk,
While others; I just bored,
Yet some; to my distress
Me, they just ignored!

Feeling the rejection of men and their kind,
I endeavoured to bend, a different way to find.
Not knowing that my Lord loves me just as I am,
Could use 'me' to express the love He can command!

Continued……

Thanking Him for this lesson,
I then had to adore;
The King and all His blessing,
So loved Him even more!

I thought I reached a plateau
With no more to learn,
So turning to serve where ere I could
His praise I tried to earn!
To find that only by Grace shall we all be saved,
All efforts buying nought,
As this debt's already been paid!

So Just as I am, I praised the living God,
Seeking for the guidance which comes from His word.
So realising His wisdom, can only stand in awe,
Find, still I love God even more and more.
I assumed I cannot love Him even more than I do today,
To find infinity to the depth, with no more I can say.

Man cannot express not in music or word,
To even try, now seems quite absurd,
Yet, as I turn to acknowledge His Glory up above;
It is then revealed that all I know of love….
Is less that God has for even one little bird.
For a single leaf which simply dies,
His capacity to embrace and nurture;
Beyond all we may surmise!

Continued……

With a thousand years to muster
All knowledge; still be sure.
God so loved us His children and His Son Jesus even more.
So shrinking in humility,
Still growing is my love.
A victim of admiration
For our Lord God above.

September 1993

## Fifties and counting

In writing these poems I call my 'Thoughts in rhyme.'
Realization of a theme is clear to find!
Obviously very green with a moral code,
Really naive, not shallow, but torn, I unload!
Anger, frustrations and expressions
My inner soul is often bared,
Exposed and vulnerable these views;
May not always be shared.
Lucky to reach my 50s and still retain something pure,
It has not always occurred to me, what's often been obscured;
That many have 'no moral compass', some really do not care.
Whilst still other souls more interested in what they shall wear.
Vandalism, bullying, many other trait's
Outside my comprehension,
Through my rose tinted glasses are;
What I have judged my views on.
Blessed by the company I have kept,
Protected from much that's real;
Many opportunities I've missed or not experienced.
To many a ' big deal.'
Perhaps we live our lives to a gradually evolving,
Grade of parameters;
Selecting what makes us comfortable
Avoiding what makes of us cheaters!
Some seek to cheat, find shortcuts and ways around, 'hedonists' I'm told.
Nothing new in this, the theme and 'lifestyle,'
Are ancient and really bold. I have decided
That even if what I believe were not all true and my faith!
These guidelines I would adhere to,
As other lifestyles against me grate!

Continued….

If Jesus were only a man,
Just some example of truth and being kind.
Even at this lower level; by association,
I am deeply glad to find;
His example is worthy of all my respect and effort to emulate.
Should we all just die and there is nothing at all beyond,
Still I prefer to stay on this path; the others seem so wrong!

Rambling on about it all; will never bring about a change,
Hot air, nothing substantial;  or even visible to rearrange.
Only a moral code, a faith, a few guide lines to hold as true,
This may appear foolish to someone stronger like you.
I don't see it as a prop, some psychological crutch!
If it was clear and easier, It wouldn't mean so much!

If a bad man had a gun on a small child
Could you watch unaffected and be ok inside?
If someone was drowning could you watch and then,
Not seek a way to help; throwing out a line to them?
Is the world better for you being a small part?
Do you help it along; appreciate each day from its start?
It has been honed in my nature, the man I have become,
No other road imaginable would I even consider to run.

It takes strength that is for sure
When temptation raised its head;
Fifty years and counting, it's not getting easier,
My eighties I dread.
Joints, tendons, forgetting little things yet aware it has gone,
Knowing you are missing lyrics, even the tune of a song.
As a singer it is quite frightening,
To have it slapped in your face,
That you are less than you once were,
Your best, gone without trace!

Continued….

Yet! Still I can't even consider being any other way,
A conscious acceptance to be as I am,
No matter what they say!
Ramblings or not, it's really quite clear;
We all have the freedom,
To select which path to take,
To which rules we shall adhere!

**Amen**?.

22 - 12 – 2012

**Relief**

Trapped in a womb, confined restricted.
Dejected, rejected, seeking to be elected!
Back into comfort, acceptance and relief.

Pressure on all sides, too busy to hide.
Options all aside, put away.
Self inflicted dues to pay,
Vulnerable and hurt,
This endless dismay.

The fight to find a reason,
As if one needs a reason.
The searching for an exit,
As if I need an exit.
The yearning for more,
But exactly more of what?
I am pushing to be released,
To be born at last, or abort.
To be free, somehow I
Endeavour to contort.
To bend and to flex, Push
Again and so perceive
That help is so close at hand!
Not some 'thing' 'We might achieve!'

Continued…..

Now I have stopped,   Long enough to listen,
Long enough to seek;   Perhaps now I'll find,
That peace and acceptance which has always been mine.
I was blind, partly by choice, to reasons to rejoice.
Defended by the **noise** of my own struggle to be free.

Then clearly it came right through,
A message, whilst not so very new,
That someone so important had unconditional love.
Forgiveness and understanding,
Even a door to God above,
The hand that came and found me,
Was strong and scarred.
The arms that reached to hold me,
With His unconditional love.
Had a permanence, security and even hope!
With all I had been seeking but with even greater scope.
So I ran towards this light,
My arms now open so wide,
I could feel this love thawing, glowing deep inside.
The immense relief, forgiveness felt within,
Why, had I waited so long to let it in?,
For now I see Jesus was there all along,
Just patiently waiting for me…To say,
"Lord, please come!"
"Come and walk with me each day,"
For I see clearly now, I was suffering for a debt,
I could never afford to repay.

Continued…….

Even though this debt is all mine,
I could never have achieved the price!
Not if I lived all my life, over and over twice!

This debt had to be paid by someone who,
Had what was required.
Someone very special and to be so much admired,
For He had bought this ticket, because;
His love was so very great,
Now I have claimed mine,
I can find that Heavenly gate.

06 – 11 – 95

For a valued and special friend.

**Musical Solution**

If music be a language where all might sing along,
Breaking down the barriers then all might sing along.
Then even little children might so plainly see,
The world is full of people, just like you and me!
To capture a melody or send out a tune,
To tell how of politics we have become immune.
It no longer affects us who is in power today,
Our problems are here and now, not so far away!

Bringing us together as peoples of **our** Earth,
All of us were children and to children giving birth.
To leaders of the future so let us help them see!
That we should work together,
To be fit, and well and free.

Breaking down barriers with music we would find,
Or any other medium to bring us mind to mind.
This opens up our world and opens up our hearts,
Just to sing together could be the very start!

20 – 08 – 84

## Man

Man who cannot make one single leaf,
But 'will' destroy entire forests.
Not one species could he create and yet appears to know less,
Than creatures of this world he helps to make extinct,
Even thought this message is quite clear and…
Really quite succinct!
With all his technology
Not one species can he make,
Nor will he ever give more than he will take!

Planet management is what we really need!
Regardless of religion, politics, race or creed.
But like little lambs we are led to the slaughter,
Will no one 'stand' the outcome to alter?
When public servants, 'Paid to serve us!'
Pass us quietly by.
No one should blame them,
For of the 'facts,' they've chosen to be shy.
In cars paid for and fuelled by the sweat of our brow,
They all look down on us, as they milk the fatted cow!
Laughing at our stupidity, mock our apparent blindness,
Leaving 'us and our children'
To face the final, awful consequence!

How long do we allow them to taint this air we breathe?
Defile our tomorrows as they wallow in their greed?
How long do we permit this deliberate destruction,
Selling our tomorrows to make their 'day's profit on?

Still 'Man' who can't replace one molecule disappearing,
Continues to watch, dispassionately despairing!
Distanced from this catastrophe by attitude unwaring.
Is he really so 'stupid' so 'vile and uncaring!'

This poses a serious question,
"Are you one of them?"
"Part of the solution or just more of the problem?"

Because….

Something between ignorance and stupidity is fine!
But knowingly and deliberately, how would you define?
The wanton and continuing destruction and waste,
Of things now gone forever….

**MAN CAN NOT REPLACE!!!**

19 – 09 – 90

Typical sunset;

St Germain De Coulamer 2003 - 2008

Filanpine Press and Publishing 2013

## True values

Strange how time seems to slip us slowly by,
Here today I'm standing with eyes cast up at the sky!
When I am sure to remember, when once so young,
All innocent, vibrant, youthful when it all began!

So willing, patient, eager to please,
But now so very often, reduced to bended knees.
Or at least so in mind; it seems sometimes as though
The world would take all I have, not even leave my soul.

True friendship for its own sake, Seems so hard to find,
Everyone just wants to 'know' In order they may climb.
That daunting, hateful ladder, To what **they** call success,
Only looking forward, never back at the mess.

Oh Lord! I know you're out there,
For I have sensed you along the way.
I've seen you in the flowers,
Oh! Even n some 'people' I should say!
In children playing, old folk quite asleep.
In all the good things my mind and heart will keep.

You who 'are' the goodness if any be in 'man!'
By this truth I will so happy stand.
Please let other of your 'son's and daughters' see,
Some **'true values**' as they are; as

**You have shared with me!**

11 – 08 - 84

## Fear, Trust and Love

So you think you have problems?
Life is hard.. you said!
Days spent in fear of nights and times ahead.
Just no material thing can console those wants and needs,
An aching deep within you on which the devil feeds.
You're not alone in this, it happens to us all.
Sometimes God is nearest, just after we fall!
It's then we ask the Father to lend a helping hand.
Some have to be humbled to serve God in this land!

Paul, who was whipped many times,
Five times thirty nine by the Jews.
Many times near death as he tried to give the news.
Three times he was shipwrecked!
Twenty four hours in the sea,
Once was even stoned.. I'm glad that wasn't me!
It takes a man of great faith to overcome all fear,
It took a man of God to stand with evil near.
So trust in God our Father, when fear has hold of you,
Stand in that light so holy; light such as Paul knew.
So help us dear Jesus sustain us when we fall,
Fill us with your Spirit that we may give our all.
In serving God the Father; of fear then rise above.
Not to be afraid; but simply **lean on His Love**.

1989

## Reoccurring Smile

On holiday we sat on a bus my wife and I,
Enjoying the views of sun, sea and sky.
A little boy was playing as he ran up the aisle
His bright eyes and teeth sparkled as his dark face smiled.

Daddy, Daddy he shouted out aloud,
All eyes now on him in the crowd.
Then as they saw to whom he ran
The 'crowd' turned away in embarrassment it seemed.
I watched him run into the 'white' couples arms!

My heart felt so pleased, my face still it beams.
When I recall this incident now twenty years along…
What was exchanged in our smiles
You could write whole books on.

28 – 02 - 96

**Avoid this mistake**

Don't touch me with your 'Bad deeds'.
Don't associate me with those base needs.
I want to hang out with the 'Wholesome seeds.'
Staying away from dangerous weeds…..
Anxious, to **not** be a part of what's evil.
Hopin' to survive; with nothin' to conceal.
No be no, insensitive, bad, cruel … heal!
But sharing the love, that's good and real.
Can't be doin' with it……… right now.
Hangin' 'round with bad stuff, gonna smell real foul!

Yeah! The world wallows in the putrid mire,
It turns away from the 'Hallowed spires'.
Seekin' only the quick buck or fix..
Gotta change, or were helping the end of it.

Can't make no other world, so what's it gonna take?
Every sister and brother please
Avoid this mistake……
If I could choose, then I'd choose 'not to loose!'
Given a choice, **dead or alive**, I choose to survive!

Why do others take such risks? They may as well slit their wrists.
Drivin' down the centre; on blind bends in mists.

Continued………..

Just takin' what they don't even really need,
Burnin' up our future to satisfy their greed.
Not seeming to care, afraid to dare, preferring to hate!
Not takin' time to nurture, solve, enable and so create.

If I could choose the right path at this speed…
The right gate in fact is what I truly need!
I don't need no hindsight for me to see,
The choice is finally mine, it begins and ends with me.

Right here, right now! Gonna make my stand!
No more this guilt, **my money, but your hands!**
I pay my dues workin' both day and night,
I expect you to 'plan' and use it right!
So take heed of my wishes and so refrain.
Don't ever do these evil things, in my name!

09 – 05 – 07

## Lighthouse beam

So many pass you by; on the bumpy road that's life.
Many become so special to you,
Like parents, children, a wife..
Just once in many millions
Who are mostly just passing through;
Comes one who is so warm and special,
Deeper, more meaningful and true.
Such as these are to be treasured
For above any material gain,
They come along beside you
In sun, wind, snow, hail and rain!
In dark days, just a thought of their tender smile,
Can carry you on and forward for a little while.
Their character, glowing can still be seen,
Not some distant, feeble glimmer;
But a girt, great 'lighthouse beam!'

Best with Phil's Cheshire accent!
Which I still hear in my head.

For my dear **friend, Phil Birchenough**. Gone home August 2012

Love to Angie his dear wife.

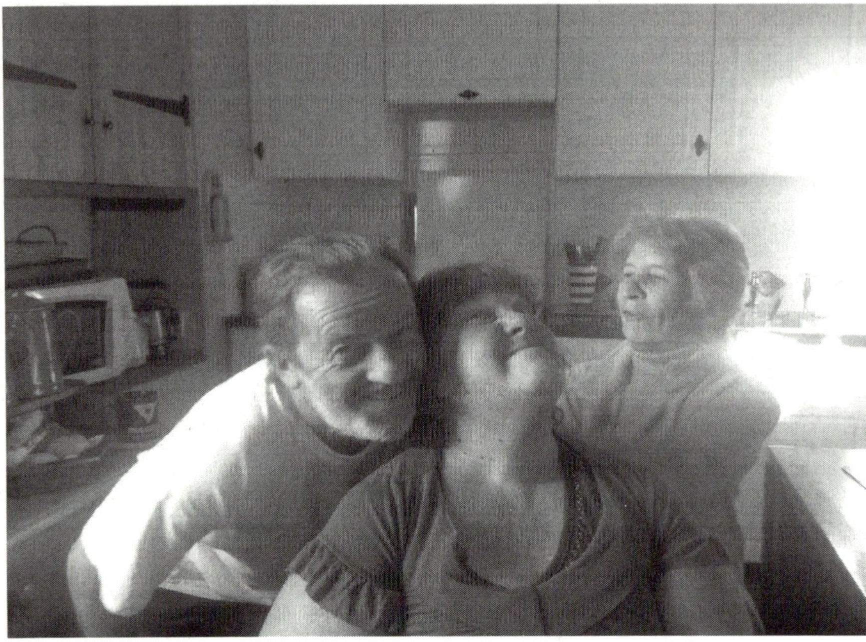

Our wonderful friend Phil, with my wife Anna and his wife Angie. Summer 2012.

Just weeks later Angie called to say he had just died, still struggle to believe it. He had a collection of lighthouses, played guitar was a sculptor, mechanic and all around gentle and kind soul. Miss him still!

## Unfailing Beauty

On balance I would rather see
A tree in all its splendour,
Early morning against lighter greens, new mown
One in particular I often ponder on!

Its branches spreading out across
Alone in the field, in which it stands,
Over thirty years have passed us by
My attention, still it demands!

Other things have turned my head
Across those years and time,
Where now those shiny cars and such
That I have wished were mine!

That temporal satisfaction
Cannot now my attention sustain,
Rather seek that which will last
Through decades of years remain.

Unchanging across my life's span
Here, long after I have gone,
Like the unfailing Love of God
This tree reflects beauty to rely on.

05 – 05 – 1999

## Cross to Bare

We all have our burdens, what, when, why and where?
Some say, "Well this is the cross I have to bare!"
This bold and brazen statement we should not take so light,
There was only the 'One' ever good enough
To bare that cross, such was His plight!

Behind that 'graphic symbol,' laid an awesome task,
An exchange for our very souls,
For which, we only have to ask!
Jesus paid with ultimate sacrifice; for even me and you,
To know this as a fact has a redeeming, lasting value.

Accepting this today as His precious gift,
That by the grace of God, beyond death you too shall live!
Not a life as we know right now
Here upon this present land,
But, rejoice for God has built far better;
Than our imagination can command.

Set your sights on heaven and all eternity
Don't consider the alternative, when all this is yours; for free.
That cross may signify 'death' to some with blinkered sight.
But after His resurrection, its significance now has new light.
No longer on that cross of wood But as Spirit, here with us all,
Yet, are we ever quiet long enough; to hear, 'His gentle call??

2nd March for Easter 2000 New life church. AOG.

**Thank you Emmanuel**

Here stands a man convicted, self-tried and judged,
Once self-opinionated yet now esteem besmudged.
When opinions were all clearer, once so well defined,
All reason in perspective. This in the past was mine.
Yet passing of time has clouded my points of view.
Not so easy a solution; more time the 'fat to chew!'
Nothing; it would appear, is quite as it seemed,
Whilst much still has so much merit;
More is less than dreams.

Reality has enchantment but ego, more demands,
A better understanding of why, where and how we stand!
If more is less, then the weak shall inherit the earth.
Less a man be born again, better his mother had never given birth.
These and other questions have often troubled my mind,
I have sensed a spiritual dimension, sought 'the path' to find!
Reason and even purpose, with guidance and relief;
Now I see more clearly 'it all hangs on one's belief!'
Belief that I am forgiven, forgiven of all crime,
Convicted, yet not to be punished,
Emmanuel, my soul be Thine.

10 - 05 – 1996 6.30 am

**Redeeming light**

On a bridge in time
A choice of path befalls,
Moist and dark out to sea;
Down streams into the dark
Morbid and daunting
Its mood shall leave its mark!

I'll choose the other path
Both 'up' and 'to the right!'
Into those trees and flowers
Up into redeeming light.

A third route occurs for both mind and soul,
One might stay right here, make this view my home.
But what is just around the bend? Up and out of view,
Seeking peace in unconditional love my Lord with you,
Curious to dance in the light of the sun
There is no choice for me when all is said and done!

April 1991

Cover photo was taken in Devon at waters meet, also inspired this poem.

**Beautiful planet; and yet!**

Smiled at a stranger, she looked at me and frowned,
Uncomfortable in a world where a smile becomes a threat!
A beautiful planet.. and yet!

A pregnant lady standing on a train,
Two young men just sitting unaware of the glares;
Their ethics and morals, yet to get;
A beautiful planet and yet!

Two grown men at a football match,
Aggressive over the outcome;
Contrast this with a man burying his son!
Lost to 'gunshot' in a war over oil;
A beautiful planet.. and yet!

Ninety percent of the world exist,
We love gently and all; just get along.
Fill the world with wonder and song
Only ten percent seek power,
Their need to control immense;
We allow them this freedom,
But they lack common sense!

Sixty years I still find it hard to understand this 'dance',
Why we tolerate this imbalance
Like we're in some dull trance.
The injustice to the weak, sick and the very poor.
We really should be doing so very much more.
What you sow in life; you then shall get,
A Beautiful planet…. And yet!

## Judge and assess

We look into eyes to read what we perceive,
Assuming and surmising then actually believe.
A spark of recognition, something undefined!
'Judge then assess' on our inadequate evidence;
Then speak just as we find!

Take time to read much deeper,
Spend 'wise' your precious love!
Earned with pure intension
Nurture **'The snow white dove!'**

Patience and tolerance magnify your 'better side'
Encourage the positive, from evil, run and hide!
It's fascination, a sparkling jewel,
Will only you 'promise satisfaction'.
Not deliver it not ever, you fool.
All fake 'glimmer' no substantial action!

Focus then on morality, lead by example,
Enlightened to encourage 'love'
Complete, pure and ample.
Dissuade others who would destroy, hate and maim.
Don't permit a minority to achieve **their master's** aim.

**Stephen and I at Box Hill circa 1962 aged 6 and 9**

**My little bruvver!**

When my earliest recollections come to mind,
Often it's my little shadow following on behind.
My little bruvver, Stephen is his name,
Unlike any other, not one ever quite the same!
A talented musician, jazz, pops to Mozart,
He still amazes me with styles from Joplin to Bach.
A master at the keyboards, he's really quite a lad!
Sinatra to Stevie Wonder, sings to make tax men glad.
He's also good at languages, 'weel jest a leetle beet!'
Back in the raving 80s was even good on his feet!
Articulate and dashing, he's even quite debonair!
His wardrobe and corbidity presented with such flair!
I only hope one day, that all the world will see;
He is undoubtedly quite special **because** he copies me!
**Just joking…** I've known him since I was only three..

So to mention someone else
Of whom we've all become a fan!
May our God bless this special union..
I present to you 'me bruvver' Stephen and…
His Belle Suzanne.

My 'Best man!' speech; for Stephen, my younger brother.

## Emotive news

At first I felt such anger
With a great big question mark
Seeking someone to blame
Who could so deeply wound my heart?
This situation is too terrible
Its repercussions too profound
The pain is too intense
Which, fond memories only compound.

As the void of loss increases,
I feel as a victim of some theft.
Someone so very special
Whose life's energy has been spilt!
Just when the last foundations
Of her life were being built.

I realise now, she was a favourite!
Someone I loved so dear,
So now I'm feeling guilty
That I didn't bring her near.
Then guilty that I didn't call.
Not even a letter sent, no invitation reminder
No time of effort spent!

Yet she new that we loved her,
That she could come to call!
She knew well of the welcome
Waiting here from us all.

She knew so very clearly
For over twenty years
Through happiness and laughter
Even tragedy and some tears!

Parents, sisters, uncles and aunts
Also many friends always engaging!
In a family with love which never ends!
All who knew her as a beautiful young woman,
Tri-lingual and so clever
A great catch for any man.

So whatever triggered, enticed her to ignore?
All those years of involvement
With those, who her, adore.
At the very peek, even edge…..
Of her new horizons,
When any moment a chance to meet,
Someone special to love and then rely on
The very best years and experiences still ahead!
Whatever can have possessed her…?
What moment of imbalance in her pretty head?
To go and cause all this grief and deepest pain!
Disregarding all who loved her,
In one leap before a train!

**Cecile Talneau 10 – 04 – 2001 aged 21**

**Foretold, forgiven, saved**

In a simple manger designed to cradle hay,
Is where they found our Jesus,
Who in mere swaddling lay.
The Old Testament foretold of the Messiah's birth,
Even to the very town of all places here on earth!
Bethlehem it said would be home to this king!
Confirmed by a star, which wise men were following.
This event depicts Christmas unto this very day,
Not presents, or Santa or some tree as many like to say!
Neither is it even merely a time of good will,
An excuse for a party or 'cash' in someone's till.

No, it's greater than man, could never imagine or perceive
The very Creator Himself, you can believe.
In Spirit now available, to anyone..
Who would  call upon His precious name.
Asking for His forgiveness,
He can comfort your deepest pain.
Promising eternal peace for your soul, and then!
Freedom from damnation, free passage to Heaven
Regardless of creed, class or nation.
Don't be misled by the general point of view,
Its fierce tide can turn your head; this is very true!
Even satisfy for a while a need or some desire.
Leaving you empty, lost, ultimately to endless fire!

Continued…..

Lord Jesus as a man, shared with us 'this Earth'!
Paid with ultimate sacrifice to our salvation giving birth,
As mediator between us and God.
No other path will ever do.

None other paying the fullest price
Has died to save just you.

2000 Bi millennium.

Two rainbows on the horizon as I drove to Sille La Guillaume one evening; remarkable event.

**Two rainbows over Sille le Guillaume Mayenne.**

**Such as eve**

Superior on the exterior
With curves and texture refined;
An ample sensual reserve
Would that it were mine!
To hold, to stroke, to share.
Moments, hours would be like heaven!
Indeed the soul would deem to aspire,
To experience such by **most men**.

Companion, friend partner and spouse,
With equality yet frail
Strength with compassion and all else they entail.
Beware any who would endanger
Harm or worse, such as these
Who are known to God by name
Each hair a precious thread
The very saints may please.

For in those days first known
When 'man' from nought was hewn!
On reflection of this experience
Who but God could have perceived!
That with some further adjustments
He might then produce
One such as EVE.

12 – 10 - 95

## Winter companions

Following Autumn which its crisp carpet has lain,
Of leaves and other debris, where woodland life has played.
Colder now and darker as days lose their vital light,
The world outside our windows, succumbs to darkest night.

Behind the drawn curtains in our private world apart,
Before a fire blazing the cat applies her preening art.
Laid stretched out before those glowing coals,
Her comfort made apparent by her purr, which grows and grows!

One glance through that window on the following frosty morn;
Reveals that snow has fallen; to carpet the dormant lawn.
A faint and haunting wind plays some baleful lament,
While we sit and recall how we, our summer's spent!

When children played in those woods which now lie forlorn!
It has become an empty place the leaves their glory gone!
Nothing, but nothing stirs;   until a little bird,
A Robin, comes to perch on a small white gate
Other birds, all flown away, but this is not his fate!
The Robin awaits the crumbs and scraps of my breakfast table,
Each winter this small companion comforts with song..
As only he is able.

November 1997

**If I were Irish**

If I were Irish; I would justly be;  so very proud!
I'd sing of shamrock and my nation's beauty aloud.
I'd take Kathleen home; back where she belongs,
No more alone in Athenrye..  so many sad songs!

Proud of the humour and so much that's so good;
If I were Irish this would be all well understood!
St Patrick happy with all the other saints;
How I would conduct myself; avoid what taints..
If I were Irish, nothing could take away
That which I felt inside, each and every day.

Eire and all she is; would be safe in my hands,
I would extend our friendship to many other lands.
The world would take notice, admiring 'my Ireland'.
Business would be secure and profits would expand
Celebrate being Irish in my mind I'd be free,
But, none who kill children and the innocent
Could ever associate with me!

So much that's good and can be shared,
While the few who bring shame to Ireland!
They bring hatred and death; don't understand
In God's name only 'love' and 'tolerance' abound!
This changing world; even worst enemies have found!
That for the children and generations to come;
Peace is worth the effort, they've put away the gun.

Continued.....

No cause on earth is worth the agony.. I plea
Justice, food and health for all and to be free!
Free to share the best things, enjoy our difference
The colour and spice they bring is immense.
The energy wasted should be put to better use,
Feeding the hungry we see daily on our news!

The modern world today should not tolerate,
The individuals who spread such death and hate.
In all its many forms it's pathetic, narrow view.
Should be alien to the likes of 'me and you!'
More positive outcomes of our endeavors
Future generations who will judge our days.
They'll wonder what we were thinking
Our debts so high, which they must pay.

When you think of how 'small' this world has become,
So much we all have in common,
When all's said and done.
Borders coming down; integration of every kind.
Better communications, the fusion of like minds.
How sad to kill over an invisible line
Pathetic to persist over the longest time!
To keep something going, because you always have.
Step back and note 'so much more to be had!
In closing I simply have to say..
Irish, or whoever...........
it's **not what defines us today**.

I am proud to come from Rye in East Sussex, but it does not define me as a human being. I love the diversity of humanity across the globe. It makes us stronger and so very much more interesting. Using this wealth of knowledge to enable the ultimate freedom, education, best health with adequate supply for all, is a goal worthy of our best effort. 05 – 01 – 2013

**By our mobile home in Lancing Beach 1989**
**Mum & Dad with their three boys.**

## The waves

Over the short wall
The waves were crashing high
Fresh and invigorating
Against the grey blue sky,
The sun lightly pouring
It's light down through the clouds;
Down onto the waves
As they smash; wet and loud!

Shafts of light peeping
Down between the gaps
Like theatre back lighting
Down; where the sea laps.
Lapping then crashing again
Smashing upon the beach,
Soaking all the rocks and stones
Both in and out of reach!

What can mere man do?
That begins to compare!
With this power and delight!
In this; so wonderful a sight?
Nothing to do but stand and admire
Draw on this strength to inspire
Praising God for His creation
Which we just have to admire!

Rottingdene sea front one lunch time 31 – 10 - 94

**Sun sets at sea are always amazing…..**

Our Tobias 'TOBY' saved from fleas and a bucket of water. Such an enormous and gentle companion as you would desire. He thought he was a dog, laid on his back all legs in the air. Had to stay in France in 2008.

## UNGRACEFUL

Pusscat sat playing cello on my floor
Your cleanliness I admire, but this I abhor
When I try and stop you
You do it all the more
Pusscat playing cello on my floor

The graceful ungraceful
Whom breathing seems to tire
The cat sat on the mat
Curled up by the fire,
Ruffles up the shag pile
Curls up her tail,
Goes to sleep after tea,
Never seems to fail.
Then as she stirs from sleep
Stretching claw and paw,
Arching her back,, her master to ignore.

Pusscat sits, and cleans herself with tongue
You think she's nearly finished,
She's only just begun.
The symbol of domesticity
With one leg in the air,
Clean yourself by all means
But don't lick your derriere
Pusscat playing cello on my floor
Your cleanliness is fine
But this I must abhor
When I cannot stop you
I'll put you out the door
Pusscat, playing cello, on my floor.

Henry Cooper who had been a true champion for the British public for so many years, had advertised 'Brut' men's after shave with the phrase.. "Splash it all over! "

He came over to us and just joined in our singing, shook our hands and was so wonderfully pleasant as to leave us being fans. Now there was a 'great British Icon and role model.'

Still sad not to have got a copy of the photo taken when he leaned lightly on my hat with his elbow, with his left hand pointing down at my face.

## Our 'Enry

What a wonderful experience in Wivelsfield Green
I could not believe, I was seeing; what was being seen!
At the introduction of the new Renault Fuego;
Which was brought in from France under covers you know!
My barbershop quartet 'Serenade' was invited to sing
We gave our very best and made those chords ring.
Other acts and stars were present to enjoy and savour
The Peter Stuyvesant ladies toboggan team in tight leather.
Jimmy Edward's brother conducted a silver band.
Captain of Sussex cricket; you could shake his hand.
We did our spot and posed for the photos and reporter
Then came a true hero 'Our Enry' 'splash it all over..!'
He stood by me about 16 inches taller,
Loved our singing even joined in a song.
Posed with me under his arm, his elbow up on my hat,
So disappointed I didn't get a photo of that.
He was the gentleman they said he would be,
Especially as he spoke to little old me!
An honour to be meeting them all, such glee!..
But I'll never forget my time with 'Our Enry!'

06 – 01 – 2013

Inspired by finding this photo to prompt a memory.

# 'J O H N S O N'

I cannot say if it is wrong or right
That we should deem to take a life,
No matter what the reason or how you work it out,
There should at the very least be no single trace of doubt.
To accuse and imprison, incarcerate, confuse
An innocent man, would not us amuse.
Only to later find that he had told the truth.
Could we sleep at night
As his body we remove.

A likeable fellow, and his family we came to know.
As the programme on our screens did unfold.
Well presented and thankfully made,
To prick our consciences,
Before the man was slayed.
Just before his family were asked to say farewell
Which is hard enough to do, in his prison cell.
They sang 'we are a family,' 'we love you always,'
And then the 'man' came,
To the end of his days,

No more 'stay' from senators, so far away,
No more time to argue, his innocence or guilt.
What's the point of crying over 'spilt milk.'
What's one life anyway, he probably killed her
Although.... I'm not so sure.
Anyway it's too late, he's gone through the door.....
In minutes it's all over, the man is history
Someone who is, now was, and it was meant to be.
The family goes home, to live out their lives,
They've done all they could do, somehow they'll survive.

Later a witness previously too stupid, or really cruel
Just 'mentions' there was reason for some doubt
And all concerned, ache as this they find out,
For now true or not, it's far too late to barter
For Johnson's dead and buried, just another martyr?.

## Trilogy

Ridged glacier rock-solid. Firmly set before all time;
Liken God as water frozen!
For the purpose of this rhyme.
Where as with water flowing
We can bathe along its brink!
Even better, immerse and absorb..
Liken this to Jesus, then deeply drink.

'Water' has its way of running,
It can 'intermingle' with man!
Freely interacting, washing, Refreshes what I am.
So vibrant then, when drinking
From that enlightened flow!
We come to understand, not assume,
But then to truly, really know!

By association with truth, we come then to learn,
That our 'forgiveness' not something we can earn.
It was purchased with 'sacred sacrifice!' Then
Through that 'living water' come to see;
Lord Jesus as our Saviour…
Claiming, 'He died for me!'
Enlightened by the 'Holy Spirit'
Which completes; this trinity,
For water then as a 'vapour'
Presents itself as steam;
God in His wisdom is all of these things.
This for now and forever
Since time; before all begins,
Simplified expression
Using ice, water then steam.

A single element with dimensions quite extreme,
Complex, yet understood even by
Children of men! It seems.
But don't be among the 'wise' during Armageddon!
For man's wisdom is foolish He presumes to understand;
But nowhere can he hide.. Not air, space or on land!

## Our Lord Emmanuel

To know a child is hungry, who would not give it food?
To know something is offensive,
Would you be deliberately rude?
In polite society or to even dare,
Have ones intent misconstrued,
Ones motives in question,
Or membership reviewed!

If as adults our responsibilities are,
To cherish and to guide those coming much later;
Then surely as nations with power too… Share knowledge
With those countries for whom.. so much; is still new!

To guide and advise them, befriend and to impart,
The benefits of our knowledge, our support at their start.
Then as with loved children who later seek to depart,
Continue to be supportive in education, business and art.

Leading by example to mutual benefit,
I can appreciate the wisdom and sense of it!
Then if a 'brother nation' is misguided or wrong,
For the 'good of the family' he must be advised,
Gently guided and persuaded until he realised;

The world is as a boat stranded out at sea,
The nations as its passengers
Comprise of both you and me.
If one should seek to sink this irreplaceable craft!
He must then be contained, for the good of all.
Even destroyed or at least put overboard!

No ransom or negotiations can be entered into,
Survival depends on us, me, them .. oh and you!
Common sense dictates the only thing to do,
Otherwise we are as animals in a poorly run zoo!

Continued…..

Man has created 'religion'
He interprets its laws,
Modified and then selected..
Boxed and then set, behind closed doors.

The Jews and the Muslims can trace their family tree,
Back to Abraham and the 'Man from galilee!'
One God for everyone, is the simple truth to tell,
He resides with us in Spirit.
He alone is Lord, Messiah and Love;
Our Lord Emmanuel.

## Sound Judgment

Be careful how you judge things,
For decisions made in haste,
Bring about disasters, ill health and waste!

Gauging situations, with too few facts,
Repeatedly creates distortion,
Leads to some really stupid acts.

In a boat out floating quietly along
In a celebration, a grand party going on!
No prior knowledge of the river, no one spied;
The rapids, risk of slaughter, so many of them died!

Life's full of decisions crossroads and choice.
Everyone has an opinion, with each giving voice.
Some taking turnings, because it looks so nice,
Often against common sense or even good advice.

Those who ignore clear signs along their way,
Even those obscured by diversion, will later pay.
So learning to read those signs become aware,
Study the directions, taking much greater care.

Maintain a vigil, with excellent 'look out'.
Open up your bible to clear up those doubts!
Be familiar with its wise teachings
For all shall be revealed; then make;
Only sound judgments in directions to take.
Loud and clear, for in God's eyes
The wisdom of men is foolish, and
It's too late to start again…. I surmise!

## Too late

Looking back on life,
In far off days to come
Will I count you as a friend?
Someone, to rely on?
Will we make things better?
Or continue to contribute to the curse?
Reducing others problems…
At least; not make things worse!

Will the world have been affected?
Anything at all improved?
Or will our deeds rejected
From history be removed?
Can we stop ozone loss?
Before it's too late?
'Wake up!' put the break on!
Only fools will hesitate!

Associate with improvements
Never adding to what's wrong!
Too many are indifferent.
Before it's too late; decide…
Which side are you on?

December 2006

## Visions of help

Taken for granted, is so much from day to day,
We walk, we talk, whether or not we've things to say.
So many major accomplishments;
But what would be our plight?
If we were to lose our senses, touch, smell or sight.

These affect us all, brown black or white!
It will never discriminate for either wrong or right.
The loss of a sense, you would not get to choose
Which affects you the most? If one 'you' were to lose!

Think on it a while
Then please give your support,
Just a smile alone can count as naught!
If I am blind, your smile, I cannot see,
So please give as you can
Please do it generously.

Much can now be done
Advances are being made,
But for research and even care
The bills are hard to pay.
In Spain they have a lottery
Supporting those who are blind!
Yet here in 'old Blighty'
We fall so far behind.
Even if just a little….
Please bare, the blind, in mind!

04 – 08 - 94

## Reap as you have sewn

I came to you one evening
It was cold and so very dark!
Black; as was my skin you were alone in the park!
Because of society and what 'it' had taught,
You rushed and passed me by leaving me with naught!

In a busy street I was hungry
Others were blind and passed me by
But you alone saw me…with compassion in your eyes!
Yet still, even knowing my plight,
You turned and walked away;
You hurt me more than those thousands
Who ignore me each and every day!

I passed you daily giving opportunity
For you to give or send;
I have never taken away your chance.
Nor shall I ever, until your very end!
There is yet still time
How long will you, from me, hide?
You may think this is your conscience,
But I am Jesus, and always by your side.

Please be more forgiving,
As you, would wish me to be…
When later before me,
I shall turn to thee.
As it has been said..
I must judge you then.
By what you have sewn in your life; which must end!
That you might join me,
In my Father's home..
When the universe together
For eternity 'we' shall roam!

05 – 08 – 95

**To the woods..  Enroute to Evron Mayenne 2006**

## To the woods

Gazing from my window
In the early light of dawn,
The view of a forest;
Trees tossed by a storm.
Just beyond the woodland,
A lakes ripples shine,
Out to hills and meadows
All peaceful and sublime.
Each day I appreciate
The colours changing hue;
Each moment vibrant,
Refreshed and sensed anew!
Never could I tire
Not from dawns early light,
To sunset through rustling trees,
Into the dead of night.
The atmosphere, the textures,
All enveloping charm,
The quiet, yet the noises, rain, wind, but calm.
Beneath this leaved umbrella,
A world set quite apart,
Yet I need not see it
For it lives within my heart,
Yet I need not feel it,
For of it I am a part.

Triggered in the night after hearing 'Richard Burton' reading
'Under milk wood' by Dylan Thomas, on the radio.
My thoughts came in rhyme for days after! Weird!

## Hot Air

The fair minded might expect all others to be fair!
But vulnerable and exposed now to those who do not care!
This, now events daily show… an increasing number,
Short sighted and self-serving; although…
Greater becomes the void between what is right or wrong
Left, right, black or white, division and prejudice
Who decides where they belong?

A century of co-habitation and tolerance
Despite the occasional dispute!
In an effort for peace and harmony,
In a mutual, Governed Europe which some might refute!
Now more free to wander, with 'evil' on every side!
Different fractions watch, then judging the rest.
With their stilted, bias knowledge, ignorant, shallow
Even just misguided at best!

These foundations laid for our next generation
Structure on which they will surely tumble,
Little co-hesion, or a shred of planning,
The bleak outcome, is that all shall stumble!

A world set apart, against itself,
All are then doomed in it to dwell;
Yet together one thing will be done!
'They'll share their journey into hell!'
Each one seeking his own solution.
Not set to seek peaceful solutions in time,
But separate, estranged,
Which will exacerbate our decline!

Does anyone else think this is a fatal crime?

October 2003

## Alpes Mancelles

Passive, unwinding, relax, peace retreat,
Lush green, inviting broad skies..
With smiles beneath!

Fragrant, often pungent, dulled senses re-awake!
So quiet and yet!
Sweet sound the birds do make.

Amble deep into forests,
O're hills with rolling views,
To dissolve into landscapes, which become of you!

Mingle, deep engrained, absorbed each into each;
Then as one united spirit, reborn!
What you learn, no one can teach..

In renewed vision with clarity,
Restored now, one's soul revived,
They who claim 'no effect!'
Are not human, or have lied!

16 – 04 - 2005

## What a shame

That a child should starve,
Brings great shame on us!
We lose a place in a queue, we make more of a fuss!
A great deal of petty waste, over indulged and spoiled,
We who are clothed and well pampered,
Play at 'work' then claim, we've toiled!

Our 'lot' is to be cosseted and well fed,
Our environment always controlled;
Never are we too hot or cold,
Hungry, thirsty or have problems that can't be solved!

Not much beyond our reach,
Some have bigger dreams for sure,
But few of us know anyone,
Who will starve to give their children more.

Who'll walk eight miles for fresh water
Every single day!
With no shoes or 'sound container'
Often then spilt along the way!
We could not survive these conditions,
Yet those who have no choice,
Deal daily with such hardships
We should give them a voice.

Be more giving; such as we shall not much miss,
Could we feed these dying children?
One less cappuccino, big mac and such
Could really do so much!
Even 60 pence a day, a few pounds
As simple as that may sound
Can transform little lives forever,
Supporting these with little endeavor.
With just cleaner water a few ounces of grain,
Some health education, lives won't be the same!
And we, well we might reduce our shame!

May 2005

## The skin you're in

We are so much less than our potential to be,
If you have not sought God's will today,
You have failed to praise His name and say…
Dear Lord, I need **Your Grace**, to you I pray!

Did you wake today and put others first?
Have you thought how to quench the thirst?
Of those millions whose lives 'you could alter?'
By dedicating funds; to provide clean water?

Have you smiled at a sad face?
Have you read the word to find some Grace?
Will you achieve some act of patience?
Will you season your day in the work place,
Enable others to see the Lord in your face?

For all fall short of the Glory of the Almighty
That is really quite plain to see,
Only through the Lord Jesus
Can we ever come into the presence of God
Through 'Grace' redeemed by His Holy Blood!

Did you think that by not doing 'evil'
You might then be saved?
Do you seek points for being 'less bad?'
If you thought you could earn deliverance
You are mistaken, so repent and be glad!

Do people know your nature
By the evidence of your actions?
Can the world see your true colours
Have you been told today, 'you are kind!?'
Do you reflect a mild, patient heart and mind?
Will a stranger smile at you in return?
In response to some inner glow;
Which carries you through a troubled world
Have you fed your heart, mind… and soul?

Continued……

Will the almighty Creator  call you by name?
Pulling you to Him, embracing His own!
Could He say, you represented me quite well!
Or turn away, leaving you to fall into hell?

Have you claimed the Saviour's sacrifice?
Will you feed your inner being?
Seeking to be owned by the winning team!
Show your colours, be the light
As salt to season all your days?
Read often the will of God, rest in His word?
Will you claim Him as your Lord always?

To not be in an active 'battle to improve'
Is thought to be; a fall into sin.
Failing to pursue a way into light….
Is just a place for us to begin.
Your humanity, character, even your soul.
Essential contents of the 'skin you're in!

After watching 'Children in need' on the BBC

# Expletives tirade

A kybosh on evolution
The world has been in decline!
Those comments on it's progress
The out come more sad, than sublime.

That one child should suffer anywhere at all
Whilst others spend a fortune in an hour at the mall.
How can so much sickness go untreated?
In a planet where a child can argue
over the colour of sheets on his bed?
The petty, shallow offspring of misguided spawn
Over spent, their lifestyle only lent
No substance to their character, abstract views
Associating with morons, too weak to choose!
Warring ignorance like an achievers badge.
Showing little evidence of any learning they've had!

Ending every sentence with, "you know?"
When it's obvious '**they**' do not!
They comment, "Do what??"
Spitting out the vulgar like something hot!
Insufficient vocabulary, patois borrowed,
In every town they talk like a lost cult.
Expletives and blasphemy used to express
Even the smallest comment, a 'foul mess!'
Through glass watch their exaggerated tirade,
It doesn't require hearing to know what's being said!
No effort to better their 'chosen reduced state'!
Love the people, it's how they act… that I hate!
Low expectations leading to a lower self-worth
We should know better, having failed them at birth.

They will be the parents of our next generation
Their example is setting the standard for our nation!
Meanwhile as we raise children in debt,
Other nations will purchase and control the inept.
As these decide which trinket shall be 'bling.'
More children elsewhere are now dying..
….. Meanwhile we?                    Now there's a thing!

## **Smokers** (Piece of 'emotive writing' as college course work.)

If an activity affects others to their detriment,
When the innocent suffer as a consequence
Even a threat to health, a decline of quality air!
Enforced dry cleaning, encouraging despair!
A habit, the result of which may induce passive cancer
Discoloration of ones décor!
A distasteful aftermath
Inducing decline in tolerance
Incurring a festering wrath!

So vile a 'personal habit!'
Should be secret and so confined'
To particular chambers
The wall should be lead lined!
No innocent party should suffer
The disgusting result,
Of another's emitances.
These culprits should be taught,
Reducing life's quality
Effecting other people's health,
Declining, even subtracting
Indirectly from our wealth!

This liberty should not be tolerated
And although this may now shock!
All smokers in a public place…
Should be taken outside and shot!

The 'brief' was to write something to read out in class which might be provocative, stir emotive argument and serious discussion. This worked!

02 – 10 - 2001

## Joys of reading

Oh! The joys of reading,
The freedom it now brings
The signs can now tell me
Which way to go and things.

The labels on the packet
Give their contents..
Even articles in magazines
Giving many 'fun moments!'

At last I can get involved
In a good bedtime story!
Reading to my children
Of postman Pat and his cat
Oh! and his big red lorry.

What is on the telly next week?
I can now understand,
Thank goodness I went back to college
For that helping hand.

Because it has changed my life
Released me from where I was before!
Today it is encouraging me
To read even more…..

For the 'Reading extravaganza' in the County Mall 1999
Attended also by Author, Mr Enfield Snr. (Harry's dad)!
I had to read this and **God's magnific trees** to shoppers.

Today it is encouraging me still.

## Fancy embroidered hat

For thirty years I have been rhyming
But the spelling was so very bad,
I could never share or show someone
This kept me quite sad,

I thought you needed
A fancy embroidered hat!
But that wasn't quite for me
At the very least,
I assumed one had to have
A university degree.

Then sending one to Prince Charles
In a bold move, I held my breath.
A letter from Buck house
Remove my mild distress

Kind words from an equerry
"His highness has asked me to convey
He appreciates the sentiments,
Also your 'enclosure' received today."
No to be seen as an endorsement
Called it not; 'your poem,'
Never the less **it's nice** and…
Something to be going on!

Kept the letter for the 'buck house' letter head as much as for the content!

## Sustain and last

Love a **mighty power** that burns inside deep,
A gift from **above** my mind and soul shall keep.
Love like an ocean; washes over me,
Taking all my hurt and setting me free!

Free from myself and the pain within my heart,
Rinse off the suffering enabling me to start….
Filling all that emptiness that swells up inside!
Takes away this burden from which I try to hide.

Take me to a fresh plain, restore my trust and faith
Die to my past pain, refresh and renew me again!
Helping me to let go of things I know shall pass,
Help me cling to the kind of thing..
That which shall sustain and last.
Hidden in a turmoil of temporal comfort and dross
Clouding my judgment; Failing to anticipate potential loss.
Warping my decisions of what is wrong or right!
Leaving me so lonely with my thoughts each night!

So Love wash over me with the power You command!
Restoring and so healing, bringing hope to barren lands.
Setting me free in pastures fresh, clean and new
Do unto to me Oh Lord, what only.. **You** can do!

In JESUS name, amen.

06 – 11 - 90

## The Queen

Working at the Savoy Hotel
Just £4-3s-6d per week
Four years well spent
Of which I'll proudly speak.

Towards the end of my training
Under chef Ironside; chief pâtissier
I learnt to make fancy pastries
With fruit, cream, even some flair.

One afternoon, after a busy morn'
Making petit fours for a special wedding
In the Lincoln suite I took them
Backing through doors that swing!

When turning then, to enter, with a tray
Nearly knocked over the Queen
I will never forget that very special day.

Her lovely beaming smile as she just stepped aside
In her beautiful gown she almost seemed to glide
Us two alone, I could have had her majesty's royal ear
All I could mumble was..
"Er, I am supposed to be here!"

Later stood outside our eyes met just once more
The car pulled away from the river entrance door
I stood by a pillar to catch one more glimpse of our Queen
I cringe as I recall now what almost might have been.
My nightmare dream, we're both covered in cream
Then as we are rolling on the function room floor!
I hear, "To the tower, Awwff with his head!" For sure!

Trainee chef; clock No 48 - 1968 to 1971

It would be so wonderful to know if her Majesty remembered this.

## Unwittingly knowing

This world is still changing day by day.
No more the paradise that it might be,
Managed by mindless greed
With some in great comfort
Many more in great need!

For years we have known cause or cures,
Even with plenty to supply
We could reduce this suffering
Yet still, we allow children to die!

Judgment on us will be so very harsh!
The earth of its balance is being mugged.
As we now sow, so shall we reap!
Truly, as we judge, we shall be judged!

When assessing what you see
Against all you understand;
This world seems so cruel, relentless in greed
Under management of man..
So much to admire in what 'he' has achieved!
But, what will those who come later see?
Will they not wonder at our 'indifference?'
To those; sick in poverty?

In the world this will be,
How will we all seem to those .. yet to come?
When we in 'hindsight are recalled!'
That even truly knowing…..
…..  still this path had run?

May 2001

Tobego beach 1998  too hot for tourists, locals played cricket nonstop for 2 hours.

We should celebrate the beauty and diversity of this world. Too many focus only on their limited politics and do not celebrate their differences, which to my mind, makes it all so very wonderful.

Phillip Robbins

## Thoughts in rhyme

Firstly I am just me I thought, as here I sat!
Nothing from before 'God,'
Can't take away from that.
Next I'm a father and a husband too!
These facts are foremost to me,
I'm proudly telling you.
But after that, I often wear a different hat,
I am an entertainer, a singer and poet too;
These are gifts, all 'given',
I had little work to do.
So in singing or reciting, I take a little credit,
A 'Christian poet' which glorifies God, I've said it!
Only after that, am I then an Englishman too,
Then European, sharer of this earth..
Like the rest of you!

We work to eat, to clothe and feed
We work to supply the children all they need.
We plan to provide a home, warmth a holiday,
Like all the other inhabitants…
Well, nearly all I say.
Most of us enjoy our lives, friends and family,
We all eat, dance, we're free to sing and play.
Free to do and go where and as we please,
Most have this freedom, I hope you can agree..
Why then do we allow a few 'troubled souls?'
To affect our existence, enforce their shallow goals?
Peace, freedom, safety with children fed and schooled.
With jobs and recreation, hospitals equipped and fueled.
So many important things, which keep us all so weary,
No time to be wasted on some 'nonproductive theory'.
Yet we impoverish the poor, congratulate the rich,
Tolerate terrorism and vandalism,
Now that is really sick!
When are we going to wake up?
So putting an end to it..

## A silly tale

Old Mc Donald sold his farm
Which was a call for some alarm!
He went to town to buy a shop
There he sold such a lot
Marmite ice cream, Now fancy that?
A very tall hat for a green fluffy cat
Bright jackets for a circus mouse
A stripy leather elephant
In a pink chocolate house.
Everything was so expensive
He didn't like to handle change
So he gave to cheeky monkeys
Who said; it tasted strange!
Mint flavoured mushrooms
Some beetroot juice with ginger
Especially developed for his niece
The classic, opera singer.
Tall shoes for those people
With very short legs
For others who eat lots of beans
Some special, nose shaped pegs.
Clockwork egg beaters
Useful tools and knick-knack's.
Including a department
For rubber screws, nails and tacks.

Now a little girl called Ruby
Who had a pony tail,
Came with her sister Grace
To buy some soap because
She had 'dippy egg'
Dripping from her face.
Toast crumbs in their socks
Jam splashed on their hands
There was jelly in their hair
A different flavour every strand.
The girls were wearing all kinds of nosh
Ruby and Grace really needed a proper wash.

Continued

So what kind of soap, did Mc Donald recommend?
Carrot juice with square bubbles?
Garden puddle water, squashed peas
With bananas in the end?
Caterpillar bogies, didn't seem quite right
So he added some purple butterflies
Which only fly at night.
But, all these things left
An awful, smelly stain,
So Ruby and Grace just walked home in the rain.
When they got home
They were both so very wet!
But everything was quite clean,
Well; as clean as they could get.

So if you need something special
Or just different, then its true
That Mc Donald's shop
May be the very place for you.
Sometimes something different
Is really worth a little try.
If you don't give it a bash
You'll never understand why,
Some people eat snails and frogs
While others eat cats and dogs
We eat cows and pigs and more
So we taste it, only to be sure
Strange things are only different
Perhaps they are **just better fried**
Because you can't say you don't like it
Until at least you've tried.

2012 Pappy's silly tale.

## Pappy

As a single man I had a degree of fun
Working abroad with days off in the sun
Life was so interesting with people and events
Around a series of jobs, to pay my weekly rent.

Then singing in a gold medalist chorus and so much more
Life got even better, with shows and concerts galore.
Meeting then my Anna, my life took a different turn
Thinking as a couple, with so much more to learn.

Took her to a few theatres just to impress her
She shared my love of singing
Thing were getting even better.

So then married with children
Those were the best of times
The travels across Europe
Our photos and films remind.

When I later became a pappy
There was even more, because you see…
Life leaped into stunning Technicolor
Exploding into; incredible **'3D!'**

Re write Jan 2013 after computer crash and lost a few originals.

## Somewhere, sometime

Somewhere no matter
What time of day or place
I shall see again and into fond embrace
That wholeness.. which endures!
The passing of all time
That which will guide me
Through those mountains
We must climb.
Sometime here after, But not for all to see
There will be waiting the one for whom I'll be
The soul and all that's in me
Forever unto to her,
And all that she desires
For all eternity.

Somewhen I'll have to leave you
Although we'll never part
Because the love you take from me
Is all that's in my heart
I want to surround you
Until you claim much more
In me is the soul you seek
Here the key to its door.
Somehow sometime
When leaves in Autumn fade
I turn to God and wonder
At all that He has made.
Amongst the things of beauty
I count you best of all;
For with the love that we now share
He answered my call.
Some how sometime
I was blessed to see
Your beauty which lies deep within
Endearing you to me
Only God so perfect
Could so create
One so very special
In you, my Anne, my mate. 01 – 11 – 92

## Concluded

Why doesn't God 'make us understand?'
Why won't he kill the devil?
With all that he commands?
Why leave us to suffer?
Undecided; on a path, that is wrong?
Distracted and so lost as we move along!

Groping in the darkness
For tiny shafts of light
Seeking out our destiny
Through long, cold, dark, nights.

Our 'free will' delaying
Our debts never paying
Our opinions keep swaying
As we reach for what is right!
You can't be made to believe
This has to be your choice
With what **you** perceive to be
Your own internal voice!

Yet God's will is so clear
He is so very, very near
Scripture holds the answers
The 'word made manifest' you'll hear.

Through a life time
You will come to understand,
That which you love, like or hate
How in different situations,
To people you will relate!
Your mind and heart will be won
Through a lifetime of experience evolution,
Once your opinion is settled
You can never be thwarted
Your salvation is then known for sure
Through faith, resolved , concluded!

12 – 11 – 98

## Measures, weights and salvation

The measure of a friend is in
How much we can trust
One who is always there?
One who might die if they must!

The weight of a problem
Can often be shared
What if it was solved completely?
By one who really cared!

The depth of true love
Now what kind one may say?
Not Eros or fraternal
Nor ever maternal, but agape!
Unconditional, all forgiving
With no bounds, for eternity
Regardless of thought or deeds,
Absolute and complete, immunity!

Such love, compassion and grace
None on earth could so impart,
Nor recreate any single thing
Or even know where to start!

The problem is that man
The very best of whom
Could be gathered up
Accumulated, then piled up to the moon.
Along with every good deed and the kindest of thought,
All counting for nothing, zilch, naught
For nothing, that truly counts; can ever be bought.

Salvation for eternity you must understand
Is the only cure, for the soul of man!
It's offered free to anyone at all
But the evil one will distract you if he can.

Continued.......

Some think they have their solutions
Islam, Judaism even many Christians
The church going religious types might
But the blind leading the blind, is often their plight!

More into their doctrines, religions and rules
A precious system or some cross studded with jewels!
Heaven awaits only those of whom
Have accepted the Lord Jesus,
Who has risen from His tomb!

As **key,** the only way to empty that portal
Accept the Grace of God now
As only He immortal,
Offers forgiveness with eternal love,
Providing the only way; to heaven up above.

**Read again those scriptures my dearest of friends,**
**Jesus alone is all sufficient**
**No one else qualifies to make our amends!**

04 – 11 - 98

## Richer than my dreams

My days were filled with endless preoccupation
Satisfying my need; for a purpose and satisfaction.
My 'nature' is to craft, working to understand!
Fashion and repair, to 'create' with eager hands.

My gifts are to master each task and undertaking,
For so many years nurturing my skills for 'making!'
Why then? Oh why? One well may ask!
Has my progress been thwarted, 'stopped in my task?'
The satisfaction of grasping new skills
Has always been 'central' to my person,
The envy of neighbours and others…
It would appear, 'me' they'd put a curse on!

Drugged like, I would fill every single day,
Seeking; things to do… 'oh! How little we will pay.
If I build it myself, I can learn and come to know!
It will only cost the materials; my 'ego' would begin to glow.

For over twenty years our home just grew and grew,
As I applied all that knowledge; both old and new.
Too many skills to list, I would turn my hand to anything
One skill led to another, then another that would bring.
To find endless evolution to our small family home
I played in a band, then 'solo' to avoid needing a loan.

Thirty years and more I toiled each week.
For over fourteen years did both and then
The second job was evenings,
So I was still free; on every weekend.

On reflection I can see;
I was high on the visual success
The results were material and evident
But my health became a real mess.

Continued……

First dermatitis was seven years of pain
I compensated by working harder, but!
My energy and strength, began to drain;

At forty one, in ninety four a result of everything
Reduced mobility, in agony, my demise was to begin!
God, in His wisdom, who knows my truest heart
Decided I was wasted; so a **change** God did impart!

I was shown that I am more than just, 'what I can do!'
I don't have to prove myself to Him, me or even you.
The loss of the freedom in doing all those things,
I thought would end my life, but no, for here it begins.

Back to school and colleges for certificates galore
Four years of gainful study, has broadened my mind
Providing new horizons too numerous to find.
Poorer by some thousands, yet richer than my dreams
In another scale and dimension, or so it now would seem!

Too close to all the detail of each daily grind
Took several hard hits to knock me back and find,
Live to work no longer.. but working then to live!
Set then; far enough back for a new perspective.
Reassess what is most important to me'
Then rebuild and enjoy a life;
Which is, inevitably; more free.

**Well! It has worked out ok for me……..**

## Zombie curse

I can't believe the human race
Has pursued its every dream
Seeking to resolve every scheme
Suffering immense pain and loss
Weighing both balance and cost!
Yet allowing the race to end up… lost!

We cannot allow evil to prevail
'Free will' and human rights
Yes, for those who tow the line
Education for all children
Leaders of the next generation
Regardless of creed, or nation.

What kind of people
Cause the innocent to suffer?
Their evil ignorance
Taking lives, not delivering souls.
For these weakest of little men
Shall be judged in the very end!
So stay in the light, avoid contamination
Hang with evil, it sticks, 'Can't build wings with bricks!'
Got to be stronger to define; 'guidelines' in rights and crime.

Breaking rules is unacceptable
This must be clear and so plain!
Ensure they are obeyed and never
Foul language, just to entertain!
Blasphemy and worse
This lack of vocabulary to express
Is like some zombie curse!

It takes care and consideration
Love and some education,
Some giving and sharing
Standing; with the positive.
Reflecting what is so true and bright;
Send 'evil' screaming, into the darkest night! 10 - 6 - 09

## The one

God is God!
The very greatest… I am.
There simply is no other
Not before, not ever, to the end!

Oh! Great and merciful creator
Many Jews and Muslims also believe this..
They would die before disowning you…
For them ok, but I'm free to seek anew.

We're told, "Put no other, before Thee!"
It is clearly written in all our text..
Save **The one** called Emmanuel
Whom God Himself promised to send!
Only He, is our Saviour.
**God's promises** shall endure; to the very end.
All other 'for me' has no allure…
Leading to 'other parts!'
Beware it's clearly written,
Lord Jesus is the only way,
To enter God's own Heaven.

This is my opinion
Based on sixty years of life,
I am happy to share this with many friends
My children and especially my wife.
It is my duty to share this as a fact
Even though many, strongly react!
I fail daily to be as God would have me be
But this failure is exactly why
I need Christ, to intercede, for me!

Mission statement and confession of faith.

## Green man

Chorus Oh green man 'tis' spring and we now celebrate
Each May when comes the blossoms We'll seek thy cheerful face,
Oh green man, Oh green man, Come hear of what we sing
Dancing 'round the merry pole A welcoming the Spring.

With friends now we all together
Many made; are all new
Joining in the merriment
Great fun for me and you.

Across the globe we wander
Yet find this ancient tale
We'll dance, share wine and song
With goodly measure of ale.

Tho' tis many have partaken
To toast this 'Man of green!'
Some even claim to have met him
But few his face have seen.

His mask it has been carved in stone
Clay and even wood
Drawn in ink or paint
But revered it's understood.

So drink up yon cider
Your beer and fine wine
Make merry with the Green man
For again tis Spring time

So when we part this evening
Our songs in mind and ear
Let's make a solemn promise
To come again next year!

Now gather we together
All those as still can..
Drink ye to coming of Spring
Sing ode to the green man.

**May 2010**

# Alpha and Omega

Alpha and omega
Beginning and the bitter end
In Hebrew, the Old Testament promised
In Greek, new scriptures now it sends
The clear paths out of darkness,
Out into glorious light.
No other way so complete
Out of that darkest night!
By no other means
Can man, come before his Creator?
So perfect is God, **our maker**!

God cannot ever look upon
Any but those; He has chosen.
Covered by Grace and His forgiveness
Only those who have come to know
Will acquire life after 'death,'
Instead of.... **terminal distress**.

Redeeming us of inadequacies
Only this brings full righteousness
The human soul must
Hail the Lamb of God and then;
As **'His children'** all then be known!
Before they can ever see; God upon His throne.

04 – 12 – 98

## Intelligent solutions

Intelligent solutions seem so hard to find,
To many of the problems **which we** in life may find
Yet some things are so clearly
Beyond personal conflict or beliefs
Above all politics and religions,
We must **now** find **some relief!**

**Relief** for children
Care for those who are sick,
Education where it is required
With power to administer it.
So the weak and oppressed can be guided to a 'better way!'
Not reliant on some 'hand outs'
Which only last a day.

In generations let others say of us..
'We' began the solution and were that vital part.
We took the initiative, ending the problems.
**With us, began that start…**

When you know you are sensitive
To opinion, view point and what is fair.
You grasp the implications from the facts
When you are not actually even there!

You sense a shared guilt
For the starving and misguided young.
You hurt for a world in self destruction
Despising its indifference, '**you** are only one!'

Others must also see these things
Which tare at a discerning heart,
Each finding their own way
To ignore, or cope. Set themselves apart!

Continued…..

Find selfish indulgencies to preoccupy
Create busy schedules, then imply..
A percentage of our earnings show that we try,
We pay our taxes that such as these shall not die!

Without our input; even more would be lost we cry.
Others just don't care, **perceive it** as **not their problem**,
Choosing to do nothing, 'we; could **start** with them!'

The balance is now all wrong
We must **all** play a part
To keep this **metaphoric horse**.
Steadily before the cart.

10 - 01 – 99 Then….

How can we always blame others?
If we don't even try to improve,
The conditions of the children
Their thirst and hunger to remove?
Dear Lord grant us the heart to…
**This 'task' begin**,
Please 'enable us' with Your Grace
To reduce this awful suffering.

Amen.

Phillip A Robbins. 26 Feb 2013.

## Epilogue

It is a pity words alone can't change the world's thinking.

There's enough in this book to feed a few hundred people.

It would be so wonderful if each book sold could feed, clothe and educate Some young soul somewhere; who could then grow up educated and healthy so intern save a few hundred more… then so on.

**In some areas just 60 pence or a dollar a day can be the difference.**

**Please consider setting up a direct debit to:-**

**'Oxfam,' ' Save the children,'** many others like**:-**
**BBC Children in Need, any that suits you.**

**Just 'please' do something, be part of the solution, not just more of the problem!**

**It is my solemn hope that some of this effort has a degree of merit, at least something of value to leave behind for those who will follow.**

**Phillip Robbins**.

**Filanpine Press and Publishing 2013**

## Eventually an end

I see beauty in every flower
I marvel at the sky
In every blossom there's a face
Over leaves sparkling with dew
Each face is the same one
An image from my memory
Never to forget; a love so very true.

(Chorus) Cool, fast water running down a mountain side
Where comes your power?
What secrets do you hide?
Let me see inside, your mind, see inside…

Every song that's sung
Of love, or from the heart
Always makes me question
The reasons that made us part
Then I began to wonder
If I'll ever love anew
Even if so, will that love be as true? (Chorus)

So God please tell me
A message you could send
Why do all the good things come to an end?
(spoken)
So flower, when you close your petals to the sky
Eventually you too
Must fade away and die. (Chorus)

I can now see, what you say of my desire
The best steel is forged in the hottest fire.
Grateful for the friends, the lessons and the strife
You were preparing me for much later in my life!

(Chorus) twice to end.

My folk song for 'Cathy' in 1969.. A Nurse at Guys.

# Thoughts in rhyme ©

**Filanpine Press and Publishing**

robbinsrest@sky.com

**Printed by LULU.COM USA**

**Put 'Diary of a Blessed man' by Phillip A Robbins In the LULU.com search engine. Then seek the Christian or Children sections for Authors Spot light and a synopsis, with more details on the Books of this Author.**

**Thank you.**

**Filanpine Design, Press and Publishing 2013**

Other books available via LULU.com:-

Diary of a blessed man — P A Robbins
ISBN 978 – 1 – 291 – 20076 - 8

Teach Yourself the Guitar — P A Robbins
ISBN 0 – 9527228 – 9 - 5

Missing you/Speedy Sam — P A Robbins
ISBN 0 – 9527228 – 3 – 6
Illustrated Childrens Storys

Coming soon.

The Golden Pyramid — P A Robbins
Science fiction adventure novel

Filanpine Press and Publishing 2013

E mail: robbinsrest@sky.com also @mail.com

Phone UK; 00 44 (0) 794 114 9304

Printed by LULU.com USA
Diary of a blessed man
by Phillip A Robbins

UTUBE:
Wheatsheaf open mic/Somehwere over the rainbow

# Diary of a blessed man
## by Phillip A Robbins

So many famous names of our generation met as I worked across Europe in the seventies including such characters from HRH The Queen to Freddie Mercury. When to meet someone famous was still an event. Then came the blessed chance to see the Caribbean and entertain around those tropical islands. These adventures were '**A once in a life time event**.' Documented here to inspire; both family and friends.

**Phillip A Robbins**